Insects
and their world

Frontispiece. Click beetles, adults of the upland wireworm, on a cereal stem

A Shell Photograph

British Museum (Natural History)

Insects
and their world

BY HAROLD OLDROYD

THIRD EDITION

London
Trustees of the British Museum
(Natural History)
1973

First Edition................1960
Second Edition...............1966
Third Edition................1973

© Trustees of the British Museum (Natural History), 1973

Publication No. 394   ISBN 0 565 053949

*Made and printed in Great Britain by
Staples Printers Limited at their Kettering, Northants establishment*

CONTENTS

INTRODUCTION

This book is intended as a simple, direct introduction to the world of insects.

We start by explaining what we mean when we speak of an 'insect', and how insects fit into the Animal Kingdom. Then we tell you the names of the *Orders*, the big groups into which insects are divided, their common names if they have one, and a little about each Order.

Chapter II is mainly pictorial, and illustrates a number of technical names that have to be used when insects are being discussed and compared with each other.

The rest of the book is an attempt to explain, very briefly, how insects live and behave, in relation to the world around them, and in relation to ourselves. To understand this we have to try to put ourselves in their place. This does not mean thinking of them as little human beings, with hopes and fears like our own. Exactly the opposite, in fact. We have to try to imagine how much, or how little, of the outside world they can be aware of with an insect's eyes, an insect's brain, and an insect's powers of movement.

Of an insect's brain-power we have hardly any idea. On the face of it, it would seem unlikely that such a small brain could have much memory, or conscious awareness, as we know them; on the other hand, the highly organised behaviour and social life of the ant and the bee are impressive, and we have yet to give a really satisfactory explanation of them.

We can only keep an open mind on the matter of an insect's brain-power, but we do know something about its simpler senses, and how it tackles the everyday problems of breathing, feeding, seeing, moving about, and so on. Chapters III, IV and V give an elementary idea of these.

Chapter VI says a little about the insect's behaviour, how it deals with more complicated problems, and how it gets along with other insects. This is a very difficult field of study. It is hard enough to explain human behaviour, when we can question the people concerned; you cannot ask an ant why it is going off in that particular direction and the most ingenious and beautiful theory may be completely untrue. So in this kind of book the most we can do is to mention a few elementary facts, and leave the explanations alone.

Few people who have not studied insects have any idea how tremendously varied they are. People generally think of insects—with a few exceptions—as rather mean and grubby things, fit only to be trodden underfoot. When you look at one under a microscope you will realise that every small part of it is most perfectly formed, every hair or bristle has its place, every joint or socket is finished off with an incredible precision. Look at the fleas in Plates 38, 39, and then remember that the whole insect is less than a quarter-inch long. A motor car is a very crude construction in comparison. Remember, too, that there are probably about one million different models (or species) of insects.

Chapter VII cannot begin to describe the diversity of insects, and has to be content with explaining adaptation, convergence and mimicry, three processes that govern some of the resemblances and differences that we see among insects.

Finally, we want to know how the insects affect us, as human beings, and Chapter VIII discusses some of the ways in which insects influence human affairs.

I am grateful to my colleagues in the Department of Entomology, for advising and correcting me in respect of the groups of which they severally have expert knowledge, and more particularly to the Keeper of Entomology, Dr Paul Freeman, and the former Keepers, Dr W. E. China and Mr J. P. Doncaster for their advice concerning the work as a whole. The Shell Photographic Unit have generously allowed us to make use of nearly a score of their photographs of living insects, a field in which this Unit has a deservedly high reputation. The New Zealand Government kindly supplied the originals of Plates 57, 58. We are indebted to the Hon. Miriam Rothschild for allowing us to use Plate 59, and to the Kenya Information Office for Plate 60. Messrs Methuen have kindly given permission for the use of several figures from Imms' *General Textbook of Entomology*, and Wigglesworth's *The Principles of Insect Physiology*, and supplied electrotypes of the original blocks. The other line-drawings in this book are by Mr Arthur Smith, and the photographs from pinned specimens were made by Mr C. Horton, formerly of the Photographic Studio of the Museum, to both of whom I am grateful for the high quality of their work.

I. WHAT INSECTS ARE, AND HOW THEY ARE CLASSIFIED

What is an Insect?

Most people, when they speak of an 'insect', have in mind any small, creeping thing, which may possibly fly, and which probably bites or stings. Zoologists use the name in a much more restricted sense, and apply it to one of the *Classes*, or major subdivisions of the Animal Kingdom: the *Class* INSECTA.

The living world is divided into two great Kingdoms, the Animals and the Plants. It is true that some organisms such as bacteria and viruses, are difficult to classify, and some others seem to be part-plant, part-animal. Nevertheless all the living things that we normally see, if they are not plants, are animals. People who speak of 'animals and birds', or 'animals and insects' are confusing 'animal' with 'mammal', a warm-blooded animal with hair or fur.

Insects, then, are animals. Each major group of animals is called a *Phylum*, and consists of animals that have the same general construction of the body, and the same arrangement of the principal organs. The Phylum ARTHROPODA gets its name from the Greek for 'jointed legs', and groups together the animals that have the outer surface of the body hardened, so that it forms a protective shell, as well as a support for the soft internal organs. This *exoskeleton*, as it is called, will bend a little in the living animal, but it is so stiff that it has to be jointed, like a suit of armour, in order to allow the animal to move about.

Arthropods, therefore, are *segmented animals*, with the body-surface divided into plates or *sclerites*, and the body as a whole planned as a series of compartments, or segments. Each segment may have *appendages*, or limbs of various kinds, which in one part of the body may be used as feelers (*antennae*), and in another as mouthparts, or as legs, or as sexual organs. The appendages, too, are segmented, with flexible joints.

Obviously an animal cannot grow while enclosed in such an unyielding case, and so the hardened outer *integument* or *cuticle* is shed at intervals in the process of *ecdysis*, or moulting. The Arthropod then grows rapidly as long as the new integument is soft and elastic: as soon as this has hardened, usually a matter of hours, the size remains fixed until the next moult. If the integument remains soft, as, for example, in many larval insects, growth may go on between moults.

1

Plate 1. A praying mantis, Order Dictyoptera, devouring a beetle-larva

A Shell Photograph

There are some segmented animals that are not Arthropods: notably the segmented worms (Phylum ANNELIDA). These do not have the skin hardened into an exoskeleton, and never have segmented appendages. In addition, there are considerable differences in the internal structure.

The Latin word *insectum*, and the Greek word *entomos* both mean 'cut-into', and so our words 'insect' and 'entomology' might have been applied to all Arthropods. By general agreement we restrict these names to only one of the *Classes* into which the Arthropods may be divided. There are eleven Classes of Arthropods, one of which—the Class *Trilobita*—is known only from fossils. Among living Arthropods the principal Classes are the following:

INSECTA (insects). The segments of the body are arranged in three groups, forming the *head, thorax* and *abdomen* (figs. 1, 2). The head has one pair of *antennae*, or feelers, and three pairs of mouthparts: *mandibles, maxillae* and *labium*—the last is a single structure, formed by fusion of a pair of appendages. The thorax often has three pairs of segmented legs, one pair on each of its segments, but never more than three pairs. The abdomen has no true segmented legs: a few primitive insects have simple appendages on the abdominal segments, and many insects, especially larvae, have unsegmented 'false legs' (*prolegs* or *pseudopodia*) (fig. 2). Adult insects often have either one or two pairs of *wings* arising from the thorax.

CRUSTACEA (crabs, lobsters, shrimps, etc.). Nearly all live in water and breathe by gills. They have two pairs of antennae, and five or more pairs of segmented legs. Other appendages may be modified for different purposes, and may be biramous, i.e. forked into two. The body may have many segments all alike, with appendages, or may be arranged in two divisions, the *cephalothorax* and the *abdomen*.

ARACHNIDA (spiders, scorpions, mites, ticks, king-crabs). These are often confused with insects, but can generally be distinguished by having four pairs of legs instead of three (young mites may have only three). The segments of the body are generally grouped into two divisions only, *cephalothorax* and *abdomen*. They have no antennae, but in their place have claws, or *chelicerae*.

MYRIAPODA (millipedes, centipedes). The name means 'with ten-thousand legs', and indeed these are animals with a great many segments, all alike, and each bearing one pair of legs; in the millipedes the segments are arranged in pairs, and so they appear to have two pairs of legs per segment.

In addition there are the Classes TARDIGRADA and PENTASTOMIDA which are small, and little known except to specialists. The

ONYCHOPHORA (*Peripatus*) are strange, wormlike creatures, which are intermediate between Arthropods and worms.

The remaining three Classes—COLLEMBOLA, PROTURA and DIPLURA—were formerly regarded as being primitive insects, but they have several structural peculiarities which suggest that they are really survivors from different lines of evolution. So current practice is to recognise four Classes: COLLEMBOLA, PROTURA, DIPLURA and INSECTA, and to group the four together into a 'superclass' Hexapoda (meaning 'six-legged') (see p. 9).

Origin and Evolution of the Insects

By anology with other groups of animals we should expect insects to have originated from a 'generalised', or 'primitive' ancestor, and to have evolved in the course of time into 'specialised' or 'advanced' types. A generalised form of a segmented animal would be one in which the body consisted of a large number of segments, nearly all of which were alike, and bore similar appendages. All existing insects, with the segments grouped into head, thorax and abdomen, are more highly evolved than this.

A number of different theories of insect evolution have been suggested, some looking for their origin among the extinct Trilobites, and some among primitive Crustacea. The theory most widely accepted at present is that the ancestor of the insects belonged to the Myriapoda, and bore some resemblance to a centipede or a millipede. It was more primitive than either of these, and most probably resembled a section of the Myriapoda called the Symphyla, which have a single pair of legs on nearly every segment.

One group of living insects is still not far removed from this ancient type. This is the Sub-class **Apterygota,** or primitively wingless insects, so-called because it is believed that they never had any winged ancestors. The most familiar examples are the silverfish and firebrat.

The great majority of living insects belong to the Sub-class **Pterygota,** or winged insects. Some insects that have no wings are nevertheless placed in the Pterygota, because we believe that they are descended from winged ancestors, and that they have lost the power of flight, and ultimately even the wings themselves, by a long process of degeneration. The reasons for this belief are firstly that their nearest relatives are a fully-winged group; and secondly that either in the adult insect, or at some stage in its development, traces can be seen of structures associated with the wings and with flight. The fleas, for example,

Plate 2. A mole-cricket, Order Saltatoria

A Shell Photograph

Plate 3. A stone-fly, Order Plecoptera

though now without wings, seem to be related to the Diptera, or true flies, and traces of wings have been reported in some pupae.

The Sub-class Pterygota falls into two major divisions, called Palaeoptera ('ancient wings') and Neoptera ('new wings').

Infraclass **Palaeoptera.** Mayflies and dragonflies are believed to be the sole survivors of two early lines of evolution, when wings—although they might have a complicated network of veins, as in figs. 4, 5—were mechanically simpler than they afterwards became. Palaeoptera cannot fold the wings back against the body, but have to hold them at rest either horizontally outwards or vertically upwards.

Infraclass **Neoptera.** All other winged insects have the wings more elaborately jointed to the body, so that they can be folded back, and lie on top of each other when at rest. This is not only tidier (compare a damselfly with a resting grasshopper or beetle), but also gives more subtle control of the wing during flight.

Neoptera again fall into two divisions:

Division I: **Exopterygota** (or **Hemimetabola**)

These insects hatch from the egg in a form already very much like that of the adult, except for the absence of wings. The wings make their first appearance as mere pads, which are visible externally, but they do not begin to function as wings until after the final moult into the adult (or *imago*).

The name *Exopterygota* refers to the externally visible wing-pads and the alternative name *Hemimetabola* to the gradual and continuous transformation towards the adult, in contrast to the abrupt metamorphosis of insects in the other Division.

The immature form of such a hemimetabolous insect is called a *nymph*. Some entomologists object to this term, either because of possible confusion with the French '*nymphe*', which means a pupa (see below), or because they consider that no clear line can be drawn between this type of development and the next one; but no convenient alternative has been found.

Examples of exopterygote insects are grasshoppers (fig. 1), dragonflies (Plate 5) and plant-bugs (Plates 10–14).

Plate 4. A may-fly,
Order Ephemeroptera

Division II: **Endopterygota** (or **Holometabola**)

These insects hatch from the egg into a form quite different in appearance from the adult, which it may not even remotely resemble. Compare a caterpillar with a moth (fig. 2), or a maggot with a fly. This immature form is called a *larva*, and it lives a life of its own, often in surroundings totally different from those in which the adult is to be found.

After moulting several times the larva enters into a resting-stage called a *pupa*, which is inactive, and most often is quite motionless. It is often protected by being enclosed in a *cocoon* or *puparium*. During this interval the body of the larva is completely remodelled into that of the adult. When the process is complete the adult breaks out of the pupal skin. The newly emerged adult insect is quite soft and crumpled, having been tightly packed into the pupal skin. For a time it is helpless, and has to spend a period, often of several hours, in expanding and hardening its body and wings.

If you see a bluebottle, for example, as it emerges from the puparium, it is almost unrecognisable as a fly. The wings are like a piece of crumpled paper, the skin is colourless and soft, and the legs are so

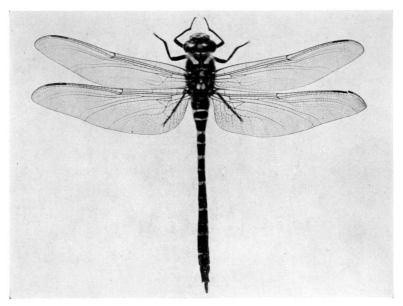

Plate 5. A dragon-fly, Order Odonata

8

feeble that the insect is scarcely able to stand. Gradually the body is inflated to its normal shape, the legs become firmer, and the wings miraculously spread themselves out until they are smooth and shining. Although this expansion may be finished fairly quickly the body is not fully hardened, and has not developed its colours fully until at least twenty-four hours after emergence.

The Division Endopterygota includes beetles, flies, butterflies and moths, bees, wasps, and ants, and many that are less well-known (Plates 15, 16, 18–49).

The Orders of Insects

The Divisions that we have just mentioned are interesting to students, but for everyday purposes we usually think of insects as being 'beetles', or 'flies', or 'dragonflies'. A group of this sort is called an **Order**, and all the insects that belong to one Order are built to the same general plan, though of course with much variation in details. The bigger Orders, like those mentioned above, are fairly easy to recognise, but if we are to classify all the rare and obscure insects we have to have about thirty Orders, and not all entomologists agree how many there should be. The list that follows is given as a convenient way of dividing up the insects and their nearest relatives for discussion, but slightly different lists of Orders will be found in some textbooks.

In the same way, the estimate of the number of known species of each Order are given so that the reader can compare the sizes of the Orders, and can see which of them are best represented in the British fauna. The figures are a long way from being final, since many new species are being discovered all the time.

Superclass **Hexapoda**

Class **COLLEMBOLA**

1. Collembola (British 250; world 2000)

Spring-tails. Small or very small, found in all sorts of moist places. In soil they can be seen in very large numbers as tiny, pale creatures, many of them capable of jumping a long way.

Class **PROTURA**

2. Protura (British 20; world 170)

Very tiny, about 2 mm long, found in debris. They are 'rare' in the sense that they are seldom seen or studied, except by a very few specialists, but they may be common if debris is extracted with a Berlese funnel.

Plate 6. A large member of the Order Psocoptera

Class **DIPLURA**

3. Diplura (British 11; world 600+)

Very similar to Thysanura (see below), and used to be classed with them. The genus *Campodea* gave its name to the *campodeiform* larva (fig. 12a), a descriptive term for all active, elongate larvae, running on three pairs of legs.

Class **INSECTA**

Subclass **Apterygota**

4. Thysanura (British 2; world 250)

Silverfish. These are the glistening, grey, wingless insects that are seen round the hearth, or in the kitchen, and which scurry away when the light is put on. They feed on starchy materials.

5. Archaeognatha (British 7; world 200+)

Similar to Thysanura, nocturnal, running about on rocks, and particularly on the shore.

Subclass **Pterygota**

Infraclass **Palaeoptera**

6. Ephemeroptera (British 46; world 1500)

Mayflies (Plate 4). The scientific name means 'living for a day',

10

Plate 7. A group of termites, Order Isoptera, mostly workers, but with
two big-headed soldiers (in white circles)

A Shell Photograph

because this is a group of insects in which the adults usually live only long enough to mate and lay eggs. The nymph lives in ponds and streams for perhaps a year or more, and eats enough in that time to supply the adult with enough nourishment to last through the short adult life. The nymphs mostly feed on underwater vegetation, and generally have two rows of plate-like *tracheal gills* on the abdomen (fig. 8).

Mayflies are remarkable for being the only insects to moult again after they have once got their wings. From the aquatic nymph hatches out the first winged form, which is covered with a fine skin and looks drab and dull; it is called a 'dun' by fisherman, and a *subimago* by entomologists. Within a day or two this dun moults and becomes a brightly coloured *imago* or 'spinner'.

7. Odonata (British 42; world 5000)

Dragonflies (Plate 5). These familiar insects are carnivorous as both nymphs and adults, and are fierce enemies of other insects. The adults catch quite big insects on the wing, and the nymphs eat other aquatic insects, tadpoles and even small fish.

There are two main groups: *Anisoptera*, the 'dragonflies' proper are generally bigger and stronger, and have the hind wings broader than the fore wings (Plate 5); *Zygoptera*, the damselflies, are very slender, with both pairs paddle-shaped and alike.

Dragonfly nymphs (fig. 9) have the mouthparts specially adapted for feeding on other small animals, including other insects, and they can shoot out an organ called the 'mask' and seize their prey. The larvae of Anisoptera breathe by means of short rectal gills, which open internally near the end of the intestine; those of Zygoptera have long caudal gills at the end of the body.

Infraclass **Neoptera**

8. Blattodea

Cockroaches. These oval insects are often called 'blackbeetles', but they are quite unrelated to the true beetles (see Order 29). The fore-wings are leathery, and act as covers for the hind-wings. Cockroaches are best known in kitchens and cellars, where they feed on scraps of food, usually at night. Wild cockroaches do occur in Britain, and the big tropical ones are often brightly coloured.

9. Mantodea

Mantids. The 'praying mantis' (Plate 1) is a slender insect, often several inches long, which has powerful, pincer-like fore-legs. It gets its name because it sits motionless in what looks like an attitude of prayer until another insect comes near, then seizes and devours it. There are nearly 200 species of mantids, mostly in tropical countries.

Plate 8. A biting-louse, or bird-louse, Order Mallophaga

10. Phasmatodea

Stick-insects and leaf-insects have the colour and shape of twigs and leaves, and can sit motionless among vegetation without being noticed. Some are big, but they are a perfect example of animal camouflage. They are vegetable-feeders.

11. Orthoptera

Grasshoppers; locusts; crickets. This Order falls into two halves, which may be roughly distinguished as those with short antennae and those with long ones. The little grasshoppers of an English meadow belong to the first group, and so do the *locusts* of tropical countries; these important pests are a kind of short-horned grasshopper, which at certain seasons bands together into a migrating swarm, and flies hundreds of miles, alighting to feed each night, and devouring everything on which it settles.

Long-horned grasshoppers (fig. 1) are soft-bodied, more lethargic insects. with whip-like antennae, and are generally found in bushes and trees rather than among grass. Related to them are the crickets and the mole-crickets: the last being powerful creatures with a big head and powerful fore-legs, with which they dig energetically (Plate 2).

Many Orthoptera 'sing' or 'chirp': the technical name for it is *stridulation*, from the Latin for a harsh, creaking sound. The mechanism is described in Chapter IV, in the discussion of hearing in insects.

12. Grylloblattodea. A small group of five species, scattered through cold, mountainous areas of North America, Japan and Russia. Apart from its rarity, chiefly interesting in linking up several closely allied Orders.

13

13. **Dermaptera** (British 9; world 1100)

Earwigs are well-known garden insects, which are mainly active at night, and during the daytime generally hide away under stones, or among plants. They have a pair of curved forceps at the posterior tip of the body, which look dangerous, but which are used for folding the wings. Many earwigs have a pair of elaborately folded hind-wings, like a fan, though few people have ever seen an earwig fly.

There is an old belief that earwigs crawl into the ears of people sleeping outdoors, and since they readily climb up into the inverted plant-pots that gardeners use as an earwig-trap, it is likely that this may be so. Two groups of earwigs have become parasitic: *Hemimerus* feeds in the fur of African rats (*Cricetomys*), while *Arixenia* is associated with Indian bats.

14. **Embioptera** (British, none; world 150)

Rare insects with no common name, which live furtively beneath stones or under bark in tropical countries. Their chief interest is that they spin silken tunnels, using silk glands in the tarsi of the fore-legs (see Chapter II).

15. **Plecoptera** (British 32; world 1500)

Stoneflies; Perlaria (Plate 3). These are soft-bodied, rather furtive insects, the nymphs of which live in clear streams and lakes. The adults do not fly much, and generally sit about among stones (hence the name), or on water-side vegetation. The nymphs may be either vegetarian or carnivorous, and have *tracheal gills* (Chapter III) for breathing under water.

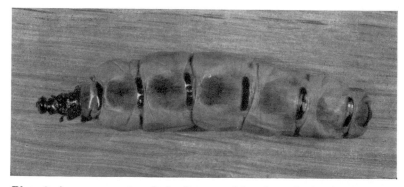

Plate 9. A queen termite, Order Isoptera. Note how the head and thorax have remained normal in size, although the abdomen is distended with eggs

16. Isoptera (British, none; world 1700)

Termites: 'white ants' (Plate 7). True ants belong to the Order Hymen-optera (28). 'White ants' are a different Order of insects, quite unrelated, and the only similarity between them and true ants is that both groups are *social insects* (see Chapter VI). This means that thousands of individuals live together in a community, and are divided into *castes*. Members of the various castes look different, and have different tasks to perform in community life.

One nest of termites may contain some thousands of individuals, and their behaviour is complex, and highly organised. Some termites live in living or dead wood above ground level, and often do a great deal of hidden damage to buildings before they are discovered. Others make elaborate nests in the soil, and may extend these above the level of the ground, to form the great *termitaria*, or 'ant-hills' that are found in tropical countries.

Termites are among the few insects that can digest wood, doing this with the help of Protozoa (single-celled organisms) in the intestine.

Like the ants and the bees, the termites group their community round an egg-laying female, called the *queen*. The queen termite has a normally-sized head and thorax, but the abdomen is enlarged into a huge bag of thin skin, packed with eggs (see Plate 9). The organisation of a termi-tarium is discussed more fully in Chapter VI.

17. Psocoptera (British 68; world 1100)

Booklice: 'psocids' (Plate 6). Very small, or even minute insects. Those with wings are rather like aphids (greenfly), but are distinguished by the pattern of the wing-veins. The wingless ones are found indoors, and get their name of 'booklice' because they are found among books and papers, in cupboards, under loose wall-paper, and so on. They are believed to feed on the moulds that grow in badly ventilated, damp places. Most of the species of this Order live outdoors in places where moulds are present, and these are called just 'psocids'.

18. Zoraptera (British, none; world 19)

These are rare, tiny insects, found only in warmer countries.

19. Mallophaga (British 250; world 2600)
  Bird lice: 'biting lice' (Plate 8).

together called **Phthiraptera**

20. Anoplura (British 36; world 250)
  Sucking lice.

These two groups of lice are conveniently bracketed together, because of their similar habits. They live entirely as external parasites; Mal-lophaga mainly on birds, occasionally on mammals; Anoplura entirely on mammals. Mallophaga have chewing mouthparts, and feed mainly on

15

fragments of feathers, skin, or other organic débris. Anoplura have sucking mouthparts, and actively draw blood from the host animal. The Human Louse belongs to the Anoplura.

21. Thysanoptera (British 180; world 3000)

Thrips. The name Thysanoptera describes the peculiar wings, which are narrow and fringed, like a tassel, though many Thysanoptera are wingless. These tiny insects, often black, can be seen on flower-heads, where they suck the sap. They feed also on other parts of the plant, and several species are recognised as pests: e.g. the Pear Thrips. Some thrips are carnivorous on other insects.

22. Hemiptera (British 1500; world 55,000)

Bugs. Though the word 'bug' is used loosely for any insect, and in the narrow sense for the Bed Bug (*Cimex lectularius*), to the entomologist a bug may be any member of the Order Hemiptera. These insects have sucking mouthparts (fig. 10d), and are divided into Heteroptera and Homoptera. Heteroptera have the fore-wings divided into two, the more basal part being harder, like the fore-wing of a beetle, while the tip remains thin and membranous; Homoptera have the fore-wings uniformly thin. In some books you will find these two groups treated as different Orders.

Heteroptera (Plates 10–12) can further be conveniently divided into land-bugs and water-bugs. *Land-bugs* include species like the Cotton-Stainer, which go from one plant to another sucking the juices, and in the process may carry the organisms of many serious diseases of crops (see Chapter VIII). Some families consist entirely of carnivorous bugs, which feed upon the plant-living insects in the same way that carnivorous mammals feed on herbivorous ones. Some may suck the blood of birds, mammals or man, and live in the nests, lairs or houses of their hosts: e.g. the Bed-Bugs (Cimicidae). Others live in the fur of bats, and suck their blood.

Water-bugs (fig. 5) again fall into two groups: the 'skaters', which run about on the surface film, and the true water-bugs. The skaters are protected from sinking by having a covering of water-repelling hairs; they feed on less fortunate insects, not so protected, which fall in and are wetted and trapped.

The true water-bugs still need air to breathe, and so when they dive they carry with them a small bubble. They often have the legs specially modified for swimming (see figs. 17a, c, e). Water-boatmen (Corixidae) eat algae and small animalcules, while water-scorpions (Nepidae) and back-swimmers (Notonectidae) are carnivorous and fierce. The last may 'bite' if they are carelessly handled.

Homoptera (Plates 13, 15, 17) include aphids (greenfly), the whitefly of greenhouses, scale insects, and a variety of soft-bodied, plant feeding bugs. The frog-hoppers, or cuckoo-spit insects (Cercopidae) and the

16

Plate 10. Adult, young nymph and eggs of the coffee bug, Order
Hemiptera-Heteroptera

A Shell Photograph

Plate 11. Head of a green mirid bug, Order Hemiptera-Heteroptera
showing the piercing proboscis
A Shell Photograph

related leaf-hoppers (Jassidae; Cicadellidae) belong here, as well as the exotic cicadas and lantern-flies, which flourish best in the tropics.

Aphids are well-known garden pests, and are even more important to the commercial grower because in the course of feeding on one plant and then on another, they carry the viruses of several dozen troublesome diseases of crops. The scale-insects have two-winged males, like small flies, but the females are without wings, and remain stationary on the plant. Often the female is covered and protected by a waxy or resinous 'scale', from which these insects get their name. Some are serious pests of fruit crops; on the other hand, the scales of an Indian coccid produce lac, from which shellac is made, and a Mexican coccid provides cochineal.

Division: ENDOPTERYGOTA

23. Neuroptera (together with Megaloptera: British 54; world 4700)

Lacewings; ant-lions (Plates 14, 16, 18). The green lacewing (*Chrysopa*) it is a beautiful fragile insect, with golden eyes, and some species come into houses at night. The brown lacewings (Hemerobiidae) are smaller and more sombrely coloured. Larvae of lacewings prey on aphids and other plant-feeding insects, piercing and sucking by means of grooved mandibles. Adult lacewings are carnivorous, and so are the adults of the related family Mantispidae, which have powerfully developed fore-legs like a mantis.

The ant-lions (Myrmeleontidae) have a remarkably aggressive and powerful larva, which lies at the bottom of a conical pit in the dust, and catches ants and other insects when they slide down it.

24. Megaloptera (for numbers see above)

Alderflies; snakeflies (Plate 19). Closely related to Neuroptera and sometimes merged with them. The alderflies are fairly large, sluggish insects. The snakeflies are more active, and get their name from the long neck and small head. The larvae of both are voracious, those of the Alderflies living in water, and having tracheal gills along each side of the abdomen (cf. fig. 8). Snakefly larvae live under bark.

25. Mecoptera (British 4; world 350)

Scorpionflies (Plate 20) are rather like a daddy-long-legs, but with a stouter body and shorter legs. They are recognised by the long, beak-like face and by the upturned tip of the abdomen in the males of one family (Panorpidae), from which they get the name scorpionfly.

The larvae of Mecoptera are like caterpillars, and the Order is related, on the one hand, to the butterflies and moths, and on the other to the true flies.

26. Trichoptera (British 190; world 4500)

Caddisflies (Plate 21). Adult caddisflies are rather like moths, but have the wings covered with hairs instead of scales. They can be found on waterside vegetation, and sometimes far away from water, especially at night, but they are not commonly met with. The larvae live under water, and most of them make themselves a 'case' from small stones and other debris, sticking it together with silk. The larvae carry their cases about when they move: they may be either herbivorous or carnivorous, and some carnivorous larvae construct a net of silk to catch other insects in the flowing water.

27. Lepidoptera (British 2200; world 200,000)

Butterflies and moths (fig. 2; Plates 22–27). Everyone knows what these look like. The wings are covered with scales, arranged in a pattern that is often very beautiful, and Lepidoptera have always been favourite insects with collectors.

For most purposes the popular division into butterflies and moths is accurate enough, though a few groups do not quite agree. Butterflies are day-flying insects, with large wings and a small body, the antennae have a small knob at the tip, and the two wings of each side are not locked together. Moths are mostly night-flying (though a few appear in daylight), with a fatter body and smaller wings, the antennae have no knob, though they may be peculiarly shaped, and the two wings of one side are generally locked together, either by a projection backwards from the fore-wing (*jugum*) or a bristle projecting forwards from the hind-wing (*frenulum*).

Another popular way of dividing the Lepidoptera is into Macrolepidoptera and Microlepidoptera, or 'macros' and 'micros'. This is mainly a grouping by size, but by general agreement some of the biggest moths go into the 'micros', because they are obviously related to the others in that section. Modern scientific classification is based on the arrangement of the veins of the wing, and on the structure of the genitalia (Chapter III), and on details of the life-history, especially of the pupal stage.

Sometimes Lepidoptera are wingless, in the female sex, though the males may have fully-developed wings: an example of this is the Winter Moth, the wingless females of which climb the trunks of trees to lay eggs, and against which greasebanding is used.

Except for the family Micropterygidae—the members of which have biting mouthparts, and are excluded from Lepidoptera by some authorities—most adult Lepidoptera have a proboscis that is adapted for sucking liquid food. Occasionally the proboscis is greatly reduced and no food is taken. We always think of butterflies as feeding delicately from the nectar of flowers, but they also like rotting fruit, wounded and sappy trees, perspiration, stagnant water, and so on.

The larvae of Lepidoptera are caterpillars, and feed on vegetation. They are distinguished from the caterpillar-like larvae of Mecoptera and of sawflies (Hymenoptera-Symphyta) by having six spot-like ocelli on each side of the head, and by the fact that the abdomen never has more than five pairs of prolegs, which are equipped with crotchets (small hooks). Caterpillars have chewing mouthparts, and eat great quantities of vegetation, so that many of them are agricultural and horticultural pests.

When caterpillars are ready to pupate, they often spin silk from modified salivary glands. This may be used to support the pupa during its resting stage, or to build a protective case, or *cocoon*. The silk worm, *Bombyx mori*, is a caterpillar that feed on mulberry leaves, and spins enough silk in its cocoon to be commercially profitable.

28. Diptera (British 5000; world 85,000)

Flies (Plates 28–37, 54). Many different groups of insects are called 'flies': dragonflies, mayflies, ichneumon flies, and so on. The true flies are an Order distinguished by having only one pair of wings (the forewings) complete and ready for flight; the hind-wings are modified into knobbed balancing organs called *halteres*.

Besides being very numerous and occurring everywhere, flies have a great range of size and shape. At one end of the Order are the daddy-long-legs (Plate 28) and midges, either very small, or fragile and long-legged, with long antennae of many segments. These are the Sub-order Nematocera. At the other extreme are the compact, often bristly flies, like the houseflies and bluebottles, fruitflies and dungflies, and so on, which, together with the hoverflies, form the Sub-order Cyclorrhapha (Plates 33, 35–37). In between there is a third Sub-order, the Brachycera, which includes such families as the horseflies (Tabanidae) and the robberflies (Asilidae) (Plates 34, 35).

The smallest flies may be 1–2 mm. long, and the biggest have a wing-span of 50–75 mm. (2–3 in.).

All adult flies have sucking mouthparts (fig. 10c). Many merely mop up liquids with a sort of sponge called the *labellum*, but others pierce and suck the blood of other insects, or of mammals and birds. Mosquitoes, horseflies and tsetse flies suck blood; robberflies kill other insects. Some families live entirely as parasites on birds and mammals, including bats. Many of these parasitic flies are wingless, as are a number of other flies that live in exposed places or in caves.

Bloodsucking flies are of great importance in the spread of disease (see Chapter VIII).

The larva of a fly is usually a grub or a maggot. Some have a distinct head, but none has true segmented thoracic legs: a few have fleshy prolegs on the abdomen, but more often these are just patches of spines, giving the larva an unshaven grubby appearance.

The larvae of many flies live in water (e.g. mosquitoes (Plates 30, 31); midges) but most live in decaying animal or vegetable matter, and the larvae of flies are one of the most powerful agencies in breaking down and disposing of organic refuse.

29. Siphonaptera (British 47; world 1100)

Fleas (Plates 38, 39). Wingless insects, flattened from side to side, and with powerful legs with which they can jump vigorously. They are small—

C

the mole flea at 5 mm. (1/5 in.) long is a giant—shining brown, and covered with spines and hairs, which project backwards, thus enabling the flea to squeeze itself forwards among the hairs or feathers of its host.

Adult fleas live entirely by sucking blood from mammals and birds. Larval fleas do not live on the host animal, but in cracks round about its home, where they can feed on organic fragments from the host's skin, and on the droppnigs of the adult fleas, which contain undigested blood. In consequence of this habit, fleas are essentially parasites of animals that have a den, a hole or a nest, to which they return frequently. Few fleas are entirely confined to one host, and they will generally breed in association with other hosts that have similar living habits: thus the 'hen flea' is abundant in the nests of a number of garden birds, as well as in hen-houses. Furthermore, adult fleas will bite and take blood from hosts on which they find themselves by chance, even if these are not their breeding-hosts.

When fleas are ready to emerge as adults from the pupa they have the peculiar habit of lying dormant until they are disturbed. Thus when people move into a house that has been empty for some time, they are often alarmed that fleas appear suddenly. This habit is clearly an advantage to a parasitic insect, because if it should emerge when there is no suitable host nearby, the adult flea might well starve before it can find food.

30. Hymenoptera (British 6000; world 100,000)

Bees, wasps, ants and allied insects (Plates 40–45). These are recognised by their membranous wings (from which they get their scientific name), the veins of which form a network of cells as in Plate 40; though in many Hymenoptera, especially the small, parasitic ones, these veins have been reduced to vanishing point.

The Order is sharply divided into the *sawflies* (*Symphyta*) and the rest (*Apocrita*).

The sawflies have no 'wasp waist' at the base of the abdomen (Plate 40), and get their name from the ovipositor of the female, which may be toothed like a saw, and is used for penetrating the stems and leaves of plants.

The larvae of sawflies are generally like caterpillars, and feed on vegetation in the same way: an example is the Gooseberry Sawfly, well known to gardeners. They are distinguished from the caterpillars of Lepidoptera by having more prolegs on the abdomen, and in particular by having a pair on the second segment.

This group also includes the giant 'wood wasps', or 'horntails' (Siricidae), which have an exceptionally long and thin ovipositor. This is used to pierce the wood of living trees, and to lay an egg within the timber. The larvae of the Siricidae burrow in the wood, and may do great damage.

The sub-order *Apocrita* again divides into two sections, the parasitic groups, and the 'aculeate', or stinging groups. The parasitic Hymenoptera (*Parasitica*) (Plates 41, 45) lay their eggs in some place where the larva,

Plate 12. Nymph of a green capsid bug, Order Hemiptera-Heteroptera,
showing the wing-pads

A Shell Photograph

Plate 13. Adults and nymphs of an aphid, Order Hemiptera-Homoptera,
on a tulip-leaf

A Shell Photograph

when it hatches, can at once being to feed on, or in, a living insect. Some choose mainly the eggs of other insects, others the larva, or the pupae, or more rarely the adult. When the parasitic larva feeds on another parasitic insect it is called a *hyperparasite*. In each case, the parasitic larva is so adapted that it gets as much food as it needs before the host insect is killed. The gall-wasps (Cynipoidea) are in effect parasites of plants, and the irritation set up by their larvae leads to the formation by the plant of swellings called *galls*.

The *Aculeata* (Plates 42, 43) are the bees, wasps and ants, some of which are notorious for their power to sting. This is confined to the female in which the pointed ovipositor has been modified into an organ for attack and defence, which can often discharge a toxic fluid into the wound that it makes. Some ants which cannot sting will bite with their jaws, and then turn round and squirt formic acid from the tip of the abdomen into the wound. Wasps and ants normally have biting jaws, and use them for feeding as well as weapons against their enemies.

Bees have the mouthparts drawn out into a long, tongue-like organ (fig. 10e), with which they suck nectar from flowers, but they still have mandibles. The leaf-cutting bees, for example, leave clear evidence of their biting powers.

The larvae of aculeate Hymenoptera are quite helpless and are supplied with food by their parents. Some solitary bees and wasps lay their eggs in holes in the ground, or in wood, provision them with a supply of honey (bees) or insect prey (wasps), and then seal them and leave them alone. On the other hand, the truly social bees and wasps, and all the ants, live in highly organised nests, with perhaps thousands of individuals, each of whom performs a particular set of duties. Social life in insects is discussed in more detail in Chapter VI.

Certain parasitic species, known as cuckoo bees and cuckoo wasps, lay their eggs in the nests of other species.

31. Coleoptera (British 4000; world 275,000)

Beetles (Frontispiece; Plates 46–49). Although this is an immensely successful group, and there are nearly as many different kinds of beetle as of all other insects together, yet most people can tell a beetle at sight. The plates of the body are particularly strong and well-jointed, and the average beetle, alive or dead, is tougher than almost any other insect.

The fore-wings are hardened into *elytra*, or wing-cases, which normally cover the abdomen, and add to the well-armoured appearance. The range of size in beetles is remarkable. The smallest beetles are less than half a millimetre long, and the longest is about 150 mm.—i.e. 300 times as long. The bulky Goliath beetle of the tropics is about 100 mm. long, so that its bulk in comparison with the smallest beetles is $200^3:1$, or 8 million to one.

Though most beetles can fly, and frequently do so, at night as well as in the daytime, they are more particularly insects of the ground, and are found most commonly in soil, among debris, under bark, and on vegetation. They have chewing mouthparts, and eat almost every possible kind of solid or semiliquid food; a few even suck blood through grooved mandibles.

Like the water-bugs (fig. 5), the water-beetles divide into those that are fully aquatic and those that merely skate on the surface. The Gyrinidae (Whirligig beetles, fig. 17d) are the skaters, and live only on animal prey. The deep-water beetles are the fiercely predatory Dytiscidae (fig. 17b) and the plant-feeding Hydrophilidae, though the larvae of both families are carnivorous. The adults of these water-beetles are fully able to live out of water, and often fly, especially at night.

Larvae of beetles are most varied in appearance (fig. 12). Many have thoracic legs, and run actively; others are white, fleshy, and curved into the shape of a letter C, and move little, others still are completely inactive, legless, and with reduced antennae and mouthparts. The form of the larva is suited to its way of life: the active ones, with legs, are generally predatory; the soft, legless larvae live on or in an abundant supply of vegetable material.

32. **Strepsiptera** (British 17; world 300)

These have no common name, though they are sometimes called 'stylopids', after the typical genus *Stylops*. They are a degenerate group, whose larvae are parasitic in other insects, Homoptera and Hymenoptera. The adult female never completely emerges from the puparium, but remains partly visible between the abdominal segments of the host. The effect of the parasitism is to cause both structural and physiological distortion in the host, which is then said to be 'stylopised'. The male Strepsipteron has wings, and is free-living.

The true relationship of these insects is not certain, but they are usually placed close to, or included in, the Coleoptera. Although they are so obscure, 300 species are known.

II. HOW THEY ARE CONSTRUCTED

We have seen already that the body of an insect is divided into *head*, *thorax* and *abdomen*, and these divisions are clearly shown in the insects illustrated in figs. 1, 2, both in the adult and in the young stages. Note that insects have no 'tail' in the true sense, because this word is used only for that part of the body lying beyond the anus, or posterior opening of the intestine. In insects this opening comes at the tip of the abdomen.

External Structure of Adult Insects

The *head* of an insect has lost almost all trace of the original segments from which it was built up. The plates that can now be seen in the head are what is called 'secondary structures', and the lines, or sutures, which mark off these plates are mostly to do with strengthening ridges inside the head.

We have already spoken of the *appendages* of a segment, which may be made to perform one of several different functions. In the head, the appendages of one segment have become the *antennae*, or feelers (see Chapter IV), of which insects have only one pair, and the appendages of three other segments have become the *mouthparts:* one pair the *mandibles;* one pair the *maxillae*, with their feeler-like *palpi;* and a third pair the single *labium*. These mouthparts have taken up a variety of different shapes in different groups of insects, according to the kind of food and the method of feeding. This is discussed in Chapter III, and several different ways in which mouthparts have been developed are illustrated in figs. 10 (a–e).

The majority of insects have *eyes* of some kind clearly visible on the head. These may be quite small and simply constructed, or they may be elaborate organs composed of hundreds of separate units. In many insects, especially some which spend a great deal of time on the wing, such as many flies and dragonflies, the compound eyes are so huge that hardly anything can be seen of the rest of the head (Plates 51, 52). The working of these eyes is discussed in Chapter IV.

The head is joined on to the body by what is called a cervical region, or neck. Some insects are stiff-necked, or have the head sunk into the thorax like a round-shouldered man; but most insects can move the head from side to side, and up and down, and also twist it round on a horizontal axis.

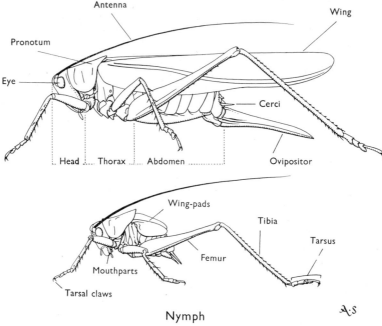

Fig. 1. A long-horned grasshopper, adult and nymph, showing the principal external features. Typical of *Exopterygota* (*Hemimetabola*), in which the immature insect greatly resembles the adult

The *thorax* shows its original three segments more clearly on the underneath, or ventral side, where the three pairs of segmented legs arise. From the upper, or dorsal side the segments that bear the wings take up most of the space in order to accommodate the big muscles of flight. Usually the second and third segments (called the *mesothorax* and the *metathorax*) are thus enlarged, at the expense of the first segment, or *prothorax*, which remains small. In the true flies (Diptera) there is only one pair of wings, on the mesothorax, and so both pro-thorax and metathorax are small in these insects.

A segmented *leg* is normally composed of five main parts: the *coxa*, or 'hip', which attaches it to the thorax; the *trochanter*, a small double-joint providing great freedom of movement for the *femur*, or 'thigh', the biggest segment of the leg; the *tibia*, or 'shin'; and the *tarsus*, or 'foot', which is further subdivided in most insects into as many as five

Adult Moth

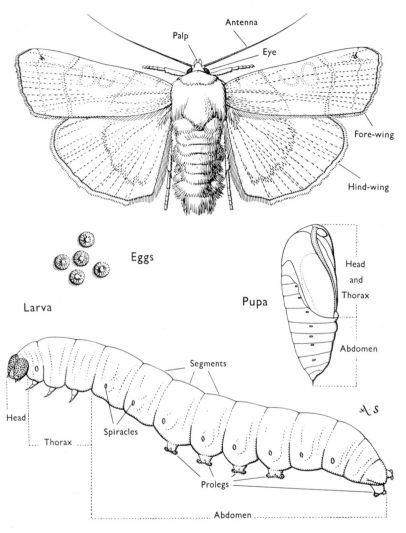

Fig. 2. A moth, eggs, larva, pupa and adult, showing principal external features. Typical of *Endopterygota* (*Holometabola*), in which the immature insect is quite different from the adult

parts. The names given in inverted commas, 'hip', 'thigh', and so on are the nearest equivalents in human anatomy. The tip of the tarsus usually has a pair of claws, and often one, two or three adhesive pads. The parts of the leg are labelled in fig. 1.

A segmented leg is primarily a device for walking or running, and for this purpose is generally slender, and flexibly jointed. A great many insects, however, use some or all of their legs for other purposes: for jumping, or swimming; or not for locomotion at all, but for seizing and holding their prey, for holding the other partner during mating, or for producing sounds. A few even use the glands of the legs to produce silk, or to extrude fluids that are poisonous, irritant or alarming to their enemies. Some of these special uses of the legs are discussed in the following chapters.

The *wings* of insects are outgrowths from the wall of the thorax, and have two surfaces pressed closely together, like a paper-bag that has been flattened. The membrane that is thus formed is supported by a series of ribs, or *veins*. One of these supports the leading-edge, and the tip, and often the trailing-edge as well. Other veins branch out from the base of the wing, and are linked by crossveins, to form patterns such as those that are well shown in Plates 19, 20.

The arrangement of these veins is not haphazard, as artists sometimes show it. On the contrary in nearly all groups of insects the *wing-venation*, as it is called, is remarkably constant, and can be used to distinguish one group from another. There are a number of systems of names or numbers for the veins, and for the *cells*, or spaces enclosed by the veins. The Comstock-Needham system of wing-venation was intended to apply to all groups, in the belief that they could be derived from one ancestral form. Space does not permit an account of this system here, but it will be found in textbooks of entomology.

The operation of the wings in flight is discussed in Chapter V.

The *abdomen* shows the original segmentation more clearly than any other part of the insect's body. Each segment normally has an upper, or *dorsal* plate, or *tergum*, and a lower, or *ventral* plate, or *sternum*, joined at the sides by a soft membrane, which allows the abdomen to expand and contract. The value of this flexibility is seen in the movements of the abdomen during breathing; when taking in liquid food, as when the abdomen of a mosquito swells with blood; when an insect stores food for the winter by enlarging its fat-body; and when the abdomen of a female insect becomes distended with eggs.

Generally the main part of the abdomen is made up of seven segments, though this number may be reduced if one or more segments have been lost, or have fused together. These segments rarely have any appendages, except in some of the primitive wingless insects of the Subclass Apterygota. The eighth to eleventh segments are generally smaller than the others, and often hidden beneath the tip of the abdomen; indeed little or no trace is left of the eleventh segment in most insects. This group of segments has appendages, which are modified into the organs of copulation in the male, and of egg-laying in the female.

There is tremendous variation in these appendages. The more elaborate forms of egg-laying tube, or *ovipositor*, may, indeed, be long and conspicuous (fig. 1), and allow the female to lay eggs in some place where they will be protected, or where the larvae will be able to find food easily—to penetrate the tissues of plants, or the crevices of wood, or to pierce the body of another animal. The highly complex male organs are less easily explained. It is not clear why some insects should have evolved such a complicated mechanism, when others can manage successfully with very simple structures. The structure of the male genitalia has been much studied because in many groups of insects the species can more easily be distinguished by this means than in any other way. Unfortunately the females of the same groups are more difficult to identify.

Internal Structure of Adult Insects

The internal structure of an adult insect is shown diagrammatically in fig. 3. The intestinal tube (alimentary canal) runs through the body from the mouth to the anus. The food is first drawn into a cavity called the *pharynx*, which has strong muscles for this purpose, and passes through the *oesophagus* or gullet, into the *crop*. In some insects this is merely a wider part of the main canal, but in others it is a bag-like structure opening to the side, and acting as a reservoir of food. The food is ground up in a *gizzard*, and then passes into the stomach, or *mid-intestine*, where nutriment is absorbed from it. At the beginning of the hind-gut, the *Malpighian tubules* act as kidneys, and discharge uric acid and other nitrogenous waste products to mix with the faeces in the hind-gut. In the *rectum*, the final section of the intestine, water is recovered from the faeces, which are then discharged as droppings from the anus.

The *blood-system* of insects is not a closed circuit like our own. Most of the general cavity of the body is filled with blood, and the so-called 'heart', or *aorta* is only a tube with valves, which stirs up the blood and gives it a sluggish circulation. The blood of insects carries food materials from the intestine to other parts of the body, and waste products back to the Malpighian tubules. It does not carry oxygen, which is conveyed directly to all the cells of the body by a system of branching tubes called *tracheae*. The construction and operation of

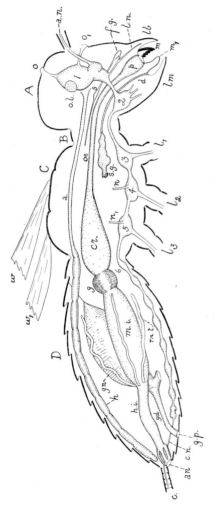

Fig. 3. The internal structure of a typical winged insect: *A*, head; *B*, cervical region or neck; *C*, thorax; *D*, abdomen; *a*, aorta; *an*, anus; *a.n.*, antennary nerve; *c*, cercus; with its nerve, *c.n.*; *cr*, crop; *d*, salivary duct; *f.g.*, frontal ganglion; *g*, gizzard; *g.d.*, gonoduct; *gn*, gonad; *g.p.*, gonopore, or external sexual opening; *h.* heart; *h.i.*, hind intestine; l_1–l_3, legs; *lb*, labrum; *lm*, labium; *l.n.*, nerve to labrum; *m*, mandible; m_1, maxilla; *m.i.*, mid-intestine; *m.t.*, Malpighian tubule; n_1, n_2, nerves to wings; o_1, median ocellus; *o*, lateral ocellus; *oe*, oesophagus; *o.l.*, cut end of optic lobe, nerve to eye; *p*, pharynx; *s*, oesophageal ganglion; *s.g.*, salivary gland; *w*, w_1, wings; 1, brain; 2, suboesophageal ganglion; 3–5, thoracic ganglia; *6*, 1st abdominal ganglion. From Imms, 1957

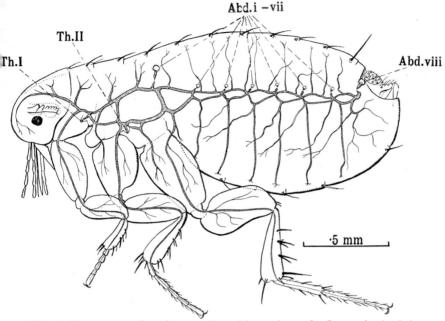

Th.II

Abd.i –vii

Th.I

Abd.viii

·5 mm

Fig. 4. The system of tracheae, or breathing-tubes, of a flea; only the left half of the system if shown. Thoracic and abdominal spiracles are indicated by numbers. From Wigglesworth, 1953

tracheae is discussed in Chapter III, along with the function of respiration. Fig. 4 shows a typical arrangement of the tracheal system in an insect.

The *nervous system*, too, is comparatively simple, and consists of a series of nerve centres, or *ganglia*, one in each segment of the abdomen and thorax, linked together in a chain by double nerve-cords running along the body. In the head these nerve-cords loop round the pharynx, and merge into a bigger ganglion which we call the 'brain'. This ganglion does serve the functions of a brain as far as these go, but it is very much less complex than the brain of even a small mammal.

In our nervous system, the brain is so very much more elaborate than any other part of the nervous system, that it clearly dominates the entire body. The insect's brain is only the biggest of a chain of ganglia, and it seems reasonable to expect that much of an insect's behaviour should be made up of automatic, reflex activity, controlled by a local ganglion, with little reference to the brain. The behaviour of insects is briefly considered in Chapter VI.

It will be noticed that the insect has its 'heart' along its back, and its main nerve-cord along its front, or ventral side; the reverse of our own structure.

Immature Stages of Insects

These have been mentioned briefly in the preceding chapter, and are discussed again in Chapter III, under the topic of reproduction in insects, so there is no need to say any more about them here.

The Size of Insects

According to Borror and Delong (1954), insects range in length from one-hundredth of an inch to more than eight inches, and in wing-span from one-fiftieth of an inch to nearly a foot. The biggest wing-span among living insects is to be found in giant moths, though some extinct dragonflies were even bigger. The longest and thinnest insects are certain stick-insects, while the bulkiest are certain beetles and water-bugs.

The beetles are remarkable in that the Order Coleoptera includes nearly half of all the known species of insects, and some of the very smallest as well as some of the bulkiest. Perhaps the smallest of all insects are some egg-parasites of the family Mymaridae (Hymenoptera).

Plate 14. An attractive insect of the Order Neuroptera, family Ascalaphidae

III. HOW THEY PERFORM THE PRIMARY FUNCTIONS

(*Breathing; feeding and excretion; reproduction*)

Every living thing, animal or plant, is a miniature chemical manufacturing plant. Raw materials are taken in, in the form of food, together with large volumes of oxygen, and the resulting chemical reactions serve three purposes. They produce the proteins and other substances needed to repair wounded or worn tissues of the body: they build new tissues, enabling the animal to grow, and to advance towards maturity (to *metamorphose*); and they release energy which produces power for the internal and external movements of an animal.

An animal, therefore, is dependent on four primary functions: obtaining an adequate supply of oxygen (*breathing*); taking in a steady supply of food (*feeding*); getting rid of the waste materials that are left over from its chemical processes (*excretion*); and providing against the day when its body is finally worn out by producing offspring to take its place (*reproduction*).

Breathing

Terrestrial or air-breathing animals get oxygen from the air round about them; aquatic animals either take down with them an air-bubble of some kind, or extract their oxgyen from that which is dissolved in the surrounding water. Vertebrate animals, including ourselves, extract oxygen from the air by means of a lung, or from water by means of a gill, and absorb it into the blood, usually with the assistance of a special substance called *haemoglobin*, which takes up and releases oxygen very easily. The blood is then pumped round the body by the action of the heart, and as it passes through the various tissues and organs these are able to take up as much oxygen as they want, and to release carbon dioxide and other waste products.

Insects also have a body-fluid that is called blood, and which carries away waste products from the tissues, but the insect blood practically never has any special substance for absorbing oxygen. It holds no more oxygen than would any other watery liquid, and as far as is known it plays only a minor and incidental part in the breathing of the insect.

Insects breathe by carrying the oxygen directly to the tissues where it is needed, nearly always through an elaborate system of branching

35

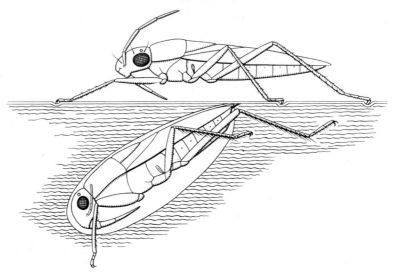

Fig. 5. Two water-bugs: a skater walking on the surface film, and a true water-bug just below the surface. The complete air-bubble shown is diagrammatic. In practice the air is carried under the fore-wings, or beneath the body, in a thin film, or *plastron*

tubes called *tracheae*. These are found in all insects except some of the most primitive wingless ones at the one extreme, and some of the most highly specialised internal parasites at the other.

A *trachea* is a flexible tube supported by an internal stiffener in the form either of a spiral, or a series of separate rings, called *taenidia:* much the same as the flexible hose of a vacuum-cleaner. Big tracheal trunks run along and across the body, and branch into smaller and smaller tracheae, then finally into *tracheoles*, which end among, and even within, the cells of the various organs (fig. 4).

In most insects, some at least of the tracheal trunks have an opening to the exterior, which is known as a *spiracle* or *stigma*. The most complete set of spiracles ever seen consists of two pairs on the thorax, and eight pairs on the abdomen, but in many insects, and especially in larvae, some of the spiracles that can be seen have no opening.

The lining of the tracheae is of the same nature as the outer skin, or integument, of the insect, as if the branching tubes were merely part of the skin that had been turned in. The cavity of the tracheal system is therefore technically still outside the body-surface, and the tracheae themselves are no more than ducts for carrying air. They do not play

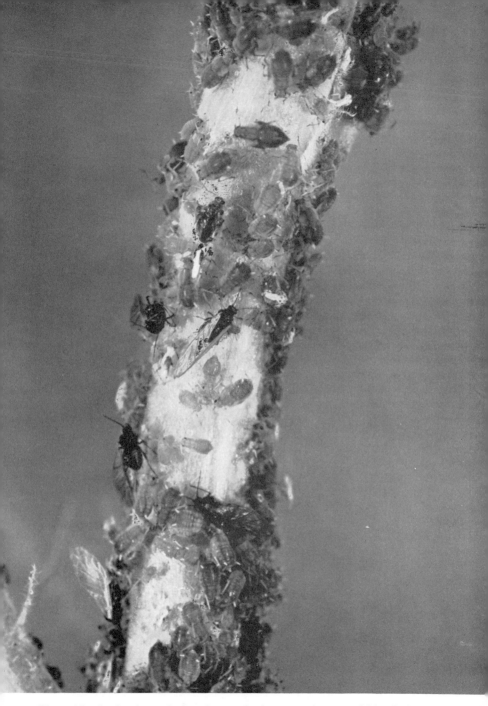

Plate 15. A closely-packed colony of the gooseberry aphid, Order
Hemiptera-Homoptera

A Shell Photograph

any part in the intake of oxygen into the tissues of the body, and should not be thought of as a substitute for a lung: the human equivalent is the windpipe, which is also called the trachea. The transfer of oxygen from the air to the tissues takes place in the tracheoles, the finest branches which have specially thin walls, and which are in intimate contact with the cells of the body.

As the tissues withdraw oxygen from the tracheoles, more oxygen diffuses along the tracheae to replace it. Diffusion alone is fast enough to supply the needs of small insects, or of bigger ones as long as they remain inactive, e.g. in the pupal stage. In active adult insects the air in the tracheae is changed by respiratory movements, particularly of the abdominal segments. If you watch a living insect you can often see the abdomen pulsating gently in this way. Many insects have *air sacs*, thin-walled balloon-like structures, which increase the volume of air on the movement inside the insect, and so have an effect like bellows. It is calculated that an insect may renew at one stroke a higher proportion of the air in its body than we can be means of our lungs; on the other hand no insect can ever be bigger than a small mammal, because there is a limit to the distance that air can be forced through narrow tracheae.

The spiracles themselves can generally be partially or completely closed. If different spiracles open and close at different moments during a respiratory cycle, they act as valves, causing the air to move through the tracheal trunks in one direction only, instead of merely moving to

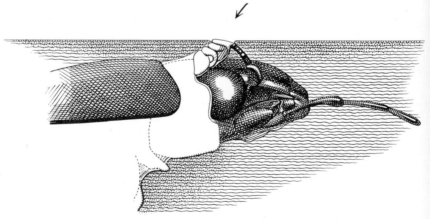

Fig. 6. A water-beetle breaking the surface of the water with its antennae (arrow), and so allowing air to flow into the bubble which it carries on the lower (ventral) surface of its body. After Hrbáček, 1950

and fro. This renews the air more completely. Furthermore, the spiracles can be closed down temporarily to reduce the loss of water-vapour from the body. The tough integument of an insect does not lose much water, but the air expelled from the spiracles carries out water-vapour, just as our own breath does on a winter's morning. In very dry climates this loss of water might be fatal to the insect if it could not be regulated.

The carbon dioxide produced by the insect escapes readily through the integument, and is not controlled by the respiratory movements.

The system just described is excellent for insects with access to un-limited air, but obviously will not work for insects living in water, or in very wet places, or as internal parasites in other animals. These must get their oxygen either by reaching to the open air with their spiracles, or by absorbing dissolved oxygen from the fluids surrounding them. Thus larvae of blowflies (*maggots*) may feed in suppurating wounds, while keeping the posterior spiracles in contact with the air. The parasitic larvae of botflies and warbleflies, living in the intestine and underneath the skin, respectively, use both methods. They take up oxygen through the skin, and also make contact with air spaces among the tissues or among the food of the host animal.

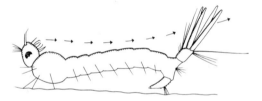

Fig. 7. The aquatic larva of an anopheline mosquito lying upside down on the bottom. The arrows indicate a current produced by the mouth-brushes, which carries minute organisms as food to the mouth, and also ensures a flow of oxygenated water over the tracheal gills at the tip of the abdomen.
After Lewis, 1949

Many larvae that live in water, or in decaying, semi-liquid organic matter, have developed a *siphon* or breathing-tube as an extension from the posterior spiracles, and use it to reach out to the air (Plate 30). Larvae of Donaciine beetles and of some mosquitoes and other flies, tap the air that occurs between the cells in the stems of water-plants, by piercing the plant with a pointed siphon.

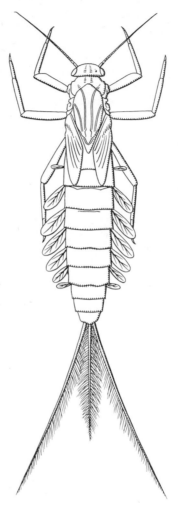

Fig. 8. The aquatic nymph of a may-fly, with leaf-like tracheal gills along the sides of the abdomen. The three long filaments at the tip of the abdomen are not gills, but act as organs of balance

Water-beetles, and water-bugs, when they dive below the surface, take down with them a bubble of air which is held in contact with their own spiracles by a cluster of *hydrofuge* (water-repelling) *hairs*. Because these hairs are not wetted the bubble is held trapped, and it serves as

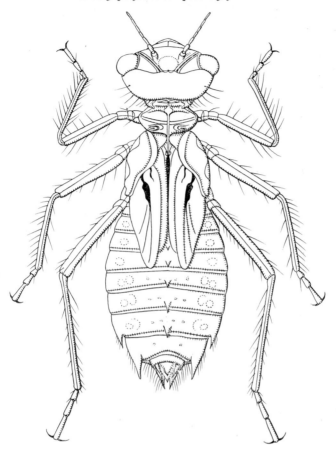

Fig. 9. The aquatic nymph of a dragon-fly, which has its tracheal gills concealed in the rectum, the final section of the intestine. Other dragon-flies (damselflies) may have three external gills at the tip of the abdomen

more than a mere reservoir of a limited supply of oxygen. Oxygen is constantly diffusing to and fro between the trapped air and the surrounding water, and left to itself would reach a state of equilibrium. As oxygen is used up in the respiration of the insect, more diffuses out of the water to take its place. The bubble thus acts as a kind of lung, extracting oxygen from the water and supplying it to the insect. A limit is set to this process, not by shortage of oxygen but by loss of nitrogen, which dissolves away in the water, and is not replaced, so that the bubble gradually gets smaller. Eventually the insect has to come to the surface for another bubble (fig. 6).

An aquatic insect is obviously at a disadvantage if it has to keep coming to the surface for air. The adult insects that do this are generally aggressive creatures, and can defend themselves. Soft-skinned nymphs and larvae are more vulnerable to attack by surface enemies, and they are generally equipped to stay below for long periods, or even continuously. To do this they have to be able to extract dissolved oxygen from the water, and to get enough of this for an active life they have to make use of special organs of diffusion called *tracheal gills*. These are thin-skinned projections from the surface of the body, either sticking outwards, or sometimes inwards into the cavity of the rectum or posterior part of the intestinal tube (figs. 8, 9). They are well equipped with tracheae, as a network of fine branches which run together, and lead into one of the big tracheal trunks. The tracheal system of such an insect is entirely closed, but it still functions in the usual way by carrying oxygen from the tracheal gill to the various parts of the body.

Blood-gills are similar organs, which have no tracheae, and which are merely filled with blood. These are believed to control the balance of water and salts in the body, and not to be actively concerned with respiration.

It is seldom that an aquatic insect relies exclusively on one method of breathing. Mosquito larvae have a posterior siphon by which they reach to the surface for air, but some mosquitoes can live entirely submerged, so long as they do not move about actively. This shows that some oxygen must be dissolved and circulated by the blood, though Lewis (1949) has demonstrated the use of tracheal gills as shown in fig. 7. It seems that the blood of insects does not normally contain any special oxygen-carrying substance, but some larvae of flies of the family Chironomidae ('bloodworms') do have haemoglobin in the blood. Here it seems to act as an emergency mechanism, enabling the larva to breathe in stagnant water, where the oxygen content is dangerously low.

Feeding and Excretion

Insects are so diverse that some group or other has learned to live on every conceivable kind of food. Among the Apterygota and Hemimetabola, where the young forms are very much like the adults, the various stages generally have a similar diet, and may live together in one colony: e.g. many of the plant-bugs and plant-lice. The Holometabola, on the other hand, may have larvae that are quite different in structure and habits from their parents, e.g. a caterpillar and a butterfly.

Whether metamorphosis is gradual or sudden, the young stages need food for growth and metamorphosis, while the adults need food for reproduction and associated activities such as mating swarms and egg-laying. Here, again, it is the insects like aphids and grasshoppers that have the easier time, because they spend their lives among their own kind, amidst an abundance of food (Plate 14). It is the insects that emerge from a pupa and then fly away that have the difficult problem of finding food in new surroundings, mating, and then returning to the breeding-ground to lay their eggs. At first sight we might wonder how the holometabolous insects came to evolve into a way of life that seems to be both difficult and precarious, but apparently the evolutionary advantages of greater mobility, and more rapid spread by finding new breeding-grounds, must offset the hazards of adult life in these groups.

Occasionally, as in the mayflies (Order EPHEMEROPTERA) and the non-biting midges (Order DIPTERA: family Chironomidae), the young form, whether nymph or larva, stores enough food to serve the adult as well, and the latter does not need to feed. It has poor mouthparts, or none at all, and its short life is devoted entirely to mating and egglaying.

Insects make use of all kinds of food, plant or animal, fresh or decayed, but their methods of feeding may be grouped into two main kinds. Either they bite and chew, or they suck, piercing if necessary to obtain liquid food. Most often all the insects of one Order are committed to one or other of these two types, even though there may be many variations in detail.

Thus ORTHOPTERA (fig. 10a) and their near relatives bite and chew at all stages, whether they are plant-feeders like the locusts, feed on scraps like the cockroaches, or catch other insects, like the mantids. HETEROPTERA (fig. 10d) and HOMOPTERA, on the other hand, all pierce and suck; mostly they suck the juices of plants, but some have adapted the same mechanism to sucking blood of other insects—like the Reduviidae, and the various water-bugs—or the blood of vertebrates—like the bed-bugs (Cimicidae) and the bat-bugs (Polyctenidae). Once again we see that the Hemimetabola, with their continuous development, generally keep the same feeding-habits in young and adults alike. The larvae of the Holometabola, living a life quite cut off from that of the adult, may have totally different mouthparts. Thus larvae of LEPIDOPTERA (caterpillars) bite and chew the leaves of plants, as any gardener knows; adult butterflies and moths have lost the ability to bite, and instead suck liquid food through a coiled tube formed from the maxillae.

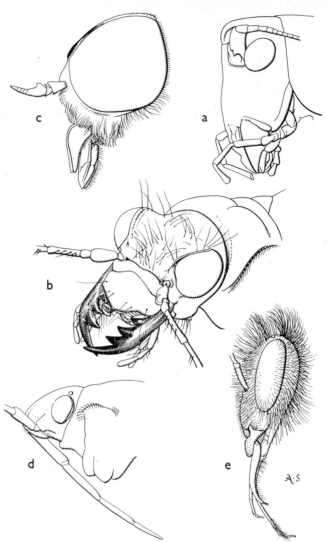

Fig. 10. Some of the different ways in which the mouthparts of insects have evolved: *a*, a grasshopper has a 'general purpose' set, with none of the components specially developed; *b*, this beetle has the mandibles enlarged into powerful organs for seizing and crushing food; *c*, this horse-fly has a soft, fleshy proboscis, which conceals sharp, stiletto-like piercing organs; *d*, this bug has a similar set of piercing organs, concealed in a segmented sheath (the labium); *e*, this bee has a soft and elongate proboscis for sucking only

Plate 16. An adult ant-lion, of the Order Neuroptera, family
Myrmeleontidae

All adult flies (DIPTERA) have a sucking proboscis, in which the
various mouthparts are combined into a tube. Most often the proboscis
is soft and sponge-like as in the housefly, and is used for mopping
up liquid food. In the flies which pierce the skin of other insects (like
the robberflies) or of vertebrates (like the mosquitoes, horseflies and
midges) the fleshy proboscis may conceal sharp, piercing stylets; or the
whole proboscis may be hard and sharp, as in the tsetse flies.

Larval flies have quite a different mechanism. The aquatic larvae
that trap organic debris in the water have modified mouthparts of the
biting and chewing type, so have the dipterous larvae that live in water
or soil, and are carnivorous; the larvae of higher Diptera (maggots) have
peculiar *mouth-hooks* with which they can tear open plant or animal
tissues, alive or dead, to release the juices upon which they feed.

HYMENOPTERA have both types of feeding in both larvae and adults.
The larvae of sawflies are caterpillar like, and bite and chew vegetation,
while the larvae of the other Hymenoptera are soft, helpless grubs,
which live either parasitically, or in a mass of food provided for them
by their parents; they therefore have reduced mouthparts. Adult
Hymenoptera have mouthparts of a chewing type, including well-
developed mandibles, but by developing the *galea* (a part of the maxilla)
into a proboscis many of them are enabled to suck the nectar of flowers
(e.g. bees, fig. 10e).

45

Beetles (COLEOPTERA) are an exception. Although they belong to the Holometabola, larvae and adults often live in much the same surroundings, and all have mouthparts of the biting and chewing type. The adults are rather furtive insects, which crawl and run more often than they fly. They have not evolved into a distinct way of life of their own, like the more aerial adults of Diptera and Hymenoptera. This is the more surprising since beetles are a phenomenally successful group, and there are nearly as many different species of beetles as of all the other insects put together.

Fig. 10 shows some examples of the way in which mouthparts may be adapted to different feeding habits.

NUTRITION

Insects need food for two main purposes: to repair worn tissues and build new ones, i.e. to grow, and to burn as a source of energy. If immature insects (nymphs or larvae) receive too little food, or the wrong sort, they may cease to grow, but many continue their metamorphosis, either at the normal speed, or at a slower rate than usual. The result is an adult that is much smaller than the average.

Adult insects of one species sometimes vary considerably in size, and people are apt to think of the small ones as being 'young adults'. In fact once an insect has moulted to the adult stage, and has fully inflated and hardened its cuticle, it does not normally grow any more, however long it may live; one exception to this rule being the mayflies (EPHEMEROPTERA), which have wings as a *sub-imago*, or 'dun', and then moult again to the true adult, or 'spinner'.

A growing insect needs proteins, carbohydrates and fats, but not necessarily a varied diet as we understand it. Many insects normally have a restricted and monotonous diet, and most insects can survive on one food if they have to.

Biting and chewing insects tear off pieces of the food they eat, and digest them in the intestine. Many insects eat leaves and other vegetation, but they are seldom able to digest the cell-walls and other cellulose-parts of the plant. Either the cells are broken open by chewing, or the contents are dissolved out, leaving the cell-walls intact. The only insects that can digest cellulose are termites, some beetles, and a few cockroaches, and they do so mostly by keeping a colony of bacteria and protozoa (single-celled animals) in the intestine, relying on them for assistance. A very few insects can themselves digest cellulose. Many insects that bore in wood do not in fact digest the wood, but feed only upon the starches and sugars that it contains.

Biting and chewing insects that live on animal protein have an easier problem, because the food material is not locked up in indigestible cellulose. Saliva is used to soften the tissues, and partly digest them before they are taken into the intestine. Many larvae that have a supply of animal food provided for them—those of parasitic Hymenoptera or of wasps—do this, and so do the larvae of blowflies, scratching at a piece of meat with their mouth-hooks.

Saliva is most efficiently used, however, by insects that pierce and suck. Plants bugs (HETEROPTERA and HOMOPTERA), of which there are a great many, push their proboscis into a leaf or a stem and inject saliva, which dissolves the contents of the cells around, without the need to break them open. A pool of liquid nutriment is formed, which is then drawn back into the intestine.

A similar method can be used to feed from other animals, and indeed some bugs (e.g. Reduviidae) have made the transition. Where the prey is another insect, the saliva can be used to paralyse or kill the prey, and also to soften and liquefy the tissues, so that the insect can be sucked dry. Carnivorous larvae of water-beetles and water-bugs do this, and so do the adults of robberflies (Asilidae) and danceflies (Empididae).

When the prey is a warm-blooded animal the food material is blood, rather than muscular and other tissue. The proboscis is stiff, and often sharp too, and either enters a blood-vessel, or lacerates capillaries until a pool of blood is formed beneath the skin. The function of the saliva of blood-sucking insects is not so much to predigest the already liquid blood, as to stop it from forming a clot which would block the proboscis or the intestine of the blood-sucking insect.

We seem to have come gradually from the feeding of immature

Plate 17. A cicada, Order Hemiptera-Homoptera

Plate 18. In the family
Nemopteridae of the
Order Neuroptera, the
hind-wings are
exceptionally long
and narrow

insects to the feeding of adults. Adult insects need food either to ripen
the eggs and sperm, or to supply energy for flight and other activities.
In addition the female has also to provide some kind of food supply in
the egg for the newly-hatched larva.

The surprising thing is that adult insects vary so much in the food
they need. As a middle group, we might take the plant-bugs and the
beetles, where the adults live a life similar to, and amongst, their young.
At one extreme from this are the mayflies and some midges, which are
able to mate, and lay eggs—and to do so most prolifically—entirely on
the food-reserves that they accumulated as nymphs or larvae. At the
other extreme are such insects as mosquitoes and horseflies, the females
of which usually need to have a meal of vertebrate blood before they
can produce eggs that will survive. Finally, the tsetse flies all take blood,
male and female alike. Now the tsetse is viviparous, and keeps its larva
in a 'uterus' of the female until the larva is fully fed and ready to pupate.
The female, therefore, has to supply the entire needs of the larva and
pupa, as well as her own: but why does the male need blood too?
Perhaps because internal feeding of the larvae does not provide a
sufficient reserve of protein for the needs of the adult alone, even
without the extra demands that have to be met by the female.

EXCRETION

The waste material to be disposed of comes from two sources. The
unused residue from the food material constitutes the faecal matter,

while chemical waste from the body-tissues themselves—arising from the breakdown and rebuilding of cells—is concentrated into urine in the *Malpighian tubules* (fig. 3). The urine and faeces are mixed in the *hind-gut*, and there and in the *rectum* (the final section of the intestine, which has special *rectal glands*) water may be absorbed, until only a dry faecal pellet is left.

The quantity of liquid that is allowed to pass out of the body to waste varies enormously in different insects. Obviously it must be related on the one hand to the amount of liquid in the diet, and on the other to the situation in which the insect lives, and whether or not it is essential to conserve moisture.

Many caterpillars, for instance, produce a dry 'frass' that is like a granular ash. Homoptera, on the other hand, produce a fluid excrement. That of aphids is known as 'honey-dew', because it contains a great deal of undigested sugar; aphids apparently swallow sugary plant juices far in excess of their needs, perhaps for the sake of some other substance that is present in minute quantities. Honey-dew is eaten by other insects, notably ants, which keep aphids as a sort of milch-cow. A similar excretion of carbohydrates by coccids on the tamarisk plant has been claimed to be the manna of the Bible.

A remarkable economy occurs in the fleas, where the larvae eat the droppings of the adults, which contain undigested blood. Flea larvae do not live on the host animal, but in cracks and crevices in its nest or lair. This dependence of the larvae on the droppings of the adults may be one reason why fleas are parasites of animals that have a permanent home, and not of nomadic ones.

Some of the chemical waste products are used in other ways, notably as *coloured pigments*. Pupae often turn black before the adult emerges, and the melanin pigment is believed to be a by-product of the chemical processes involved. The pigments that contribute to the pattern of butterflies and other insects seem to be part of the chemical process, too, but many of the most brilliant colours seen in insects, especially in beetles, are not pigments. They are an iridescence caused by the optical interference that arises when the surface of the body is covered with very fine markings.

Reproduction

Insects are bi-sexual, and have distinct male and female individuals; unlike snails or worms, where one individual may be both male and female, either at the same time, or consecutively.

The normal sequence of events is that the male transfers sperm to the female by means of an intromittent organ, or *penis*. Within the

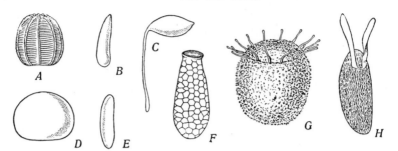

Fig. 11. Eggs of various insects: *A*, a butterfly; *B*, the House Fly; *C*, a chalcid; *D*, a butterfly; *E*, a gall-midge; *F*, *G*, plant-bugs: H, a small fruit fly. Greatly magnified. From Imms, 1957

female the sperm is stored in a *spermatheca* or *receptaculum seminis*, so making it possible for eggs to be fertilised for a considerable time after mating has taken place. The queens of bees and ants, for example, may take part in a mating-flight only once, but go on laying fertile eggs throughout their life.

Reproduction from unfertilised eggs is called *parthenogenesis*, and occurs now and then in most groups of insects. In the aphids and in the gall-wasps (Hymenoptera; Cynipoidea) it is normal for one or more generations each year to consist of females only, and to be parthenogenetic. This occurs in the Spring, and may be one of the reasons why these insects can increase so rapidly and disastrously in a favourable year. Honey-bees produce females from fertilised eggs, and males (drones) from unfertilised ones.

EGG-LAYING

The eggs are formed in *ovarioles*, or egg-tubes, of which there are normally two bunches, each united at the base into an *oviduct* (fig. 3gd). Eggs form near the tip of each ovariole, and move down as they grow. On the way down they receive their store of food from nutritive cells, but the mechanism by which this occurs varies greatly in different groups of insects, some of which have no nutritive cells at all.

The eggs pass down the oviduct into a single cavity called the *vagina*, and here they receive the sperm from the spermatheca, which we have already mentioned. The fertilised egg then passes on and out. In insects that lay eggs in a steady stream as soon as they are fertilised, the vagina is a simple tube. The tsetse fly, which hatches the egg internally and then feeds the larva until it is fully grown before releasing it, has the vagina enlarged into a *uterus*.

50

Plate 19. A snake-fly, Order Megaloptera

The external opening, or *ovipositor*, through which the eggs are expelled varies greatly in different groups of insects, and its shape reveals not so much the relationships of the insect as its breeding habits. The appendages of the eighth and ninth segments of the abdomen—i.e. the structures that on the head have become antennae and mouthparts, and on the thorax have become legs—are modified into lobes and valves to guide the egg on its way out. A simple arrangement suffices for all insects that merely drop the eggs on to the ground, among vegetation, or into water: and even for some that place the eggs carefully in a neat stack, e.g. butterflies, mosquitoes, horseflies.

The ORTHOPTERA show how this simple ovipositor can be adapted for different uses. The locusts and short-horned grasshoppers merely have the valves of the ovipositor short and strong, and use them to open a way into the soil. The greater part of the abdomen is pushed into the ground, and the eggs are laid at the bottom of the pit. The long-horned grasshoppers, however, have the valves of the ovipositor drawn out into long blades, which interlock and form a compound piercing organ of great strength (fig. 1). This may be used to pierce the soil, also, but the purpose for which it is adapted seems to be to push into the wrapped tissues of plants, so as to lay eggs between the layers. At the other end of the evolutionary scale of insects, among the DIPTERA, or true flies, there are some that have a flattened, blade-like ovipositor that is used in much the same way.

51

It is in the HYMENOPTERA that the ovipositor reaches its most complex development. The valves of the eighth and ninth segments are often long and thin, and elaborately locked together. In the sawflies (SYMPHYTA) the blades are often toothed, and are used alternately to saw a way into leaves and stems. The giant wood-wasps have a very long, thin, but strong ovipositor, which is used as an auger to bore through the bark of trees, and to lay eggs in the wood, one egg in each hole. An ichneumon (*Rhyssa*) breeds as a parasite of the wood-wasp larvae, and is equipped with an ovipositor of a comparable length with which to reach them.

Other ichneumon flies use their long ovipositor to lay eggs inside other insect larva, particularly the caterpillars of butterflies and moths. The ichneumon larva feeds internally, eventually killing the host or victim. Other smaller parasitic Hymenoptera lay eggs in the eggs of other insects, and have comparatively short ovipositors.

Wasps and bees have gone further, and use the valves of the eighth and ninth segments as a *sting*. Besides inflicting pain by the piercing action of the sting, they are equipped with poison glands which allow a powerful irritant liquid to be injected into the wound. Ants can both sting and bite, and so like horses are dangerous at both ends. The

Plate 20. A scorpion-fly, Order Mecoptera, with the turned-up tip of the abdomen from which it gets its name

sting sometimes has barbs, similar to the saw-teeth of the sawflies, and in the honey-bee and some others these barbs are so big that the sting is left behind if it enters the human skin.

The *eggs* of insects may be of almost any shape, from a sausage to a sphere, or a disc (fig. 11). Some rounded ones are flattened on one side, where they stick to a surface. There is no certain way of distinguishing them from the eggs of other invertebrate animals, but since there are more different kinds of insects than there are of all other animals together, you will most often be safe in assuming that any small eggs that you find are probably those of an insect.

Some insects produce only one egg at a time; others, like the queens of the bees and termites, become mere egg-laying machines, and produce hundreds, or thousands of eggs over a period of time.

Many insects merely drop their eggs, either scattering them at random, or dropping them into a mass of material that is suitable for the larvae to feed on: e.g. dung, rotting vegetable or animal materials, or fruit. Those whose larvae live among vegetation may attach their eggs to leaves or stems (Plate 50), often to the underside of a leaf where they will not be easily seen by enemies. If the larvae are going to live in water, the eggs may be found attached to plants standing in, or overhanging ponds and streams. The eggs of the lacewing, *Chrysopa*, are each attached to a plant by a fine thread, which hardens quickly into a thin stalk.

The eggs of parasitic insects are usually laid in, on or near to a suitable host, and those with carnivorous larvae may be laid near a store of food: Hymenoptera provide examples of both groups.

There are various ways in which the eggs may be protected. Many ORTHOPTERA enclose a batch of eggs in a pod (or *ootheca*), which may be buried in the ground. Some HOMOPTERA, especially Fulgoroidea ('lantern-flies'), cover their eggs with wax filaments. We have already mentioned woodboring insects, which insert their eggs into the wood, and their parasites, which follow them there.

The *embryology* of insects, that is their development from a single cell into a larvae that can live independently, is outside the scope of the present work. It is treated in detail in the Textbooks of Entomology.

When the larva is ready to hatch it breaks through the egg-shell mainly by pushing hard. The shell has certain lines of weakness along which it is easily split, and many larvae have so-called 'egg-bursters' to help them to do this. These are projections, usually on the head which seem to exist only for this moment. They do not so much slit the egg-shell, as prick it like a balloon, whereupon it flies apart.

Normally only one larva hatches from each egg, but in a few insects

Plate 21. A caddis-fly, Order Trichoptera, with hairy wings

the single fertilised ovum may give rise to two or more embryos: perhaps to a great number. *Polyembryony*, as it is called, is highly developed in parasitic Hymenoptera, where as many as a thousand larvae may arise from one egg. A parasitic insect is handicapped by having to find a suitable host in which to lay its eggs, and there must be very many failures: a device such as polyembryony may perhaps help to restore the balance of numbers.

At the opposite end of the scale a few insects, notably the tsetse flies and certain other flies known as Pupipara, do not lay eggs but hatch one egg at a time internally and feed a single larva upon internal secretions until it is ready to pupate.

NYMPHS AND LARVAE

These names have been explained earlier in this work, along with the process of metamorphosis by successive moults. Each of the periods between moults is called a *stadium*, and the insect itself during a given stadium is called an *instar:* '1st instar nymph', '3rd instar larva' and so on.

The number of instars varies from two to more than fifty, and

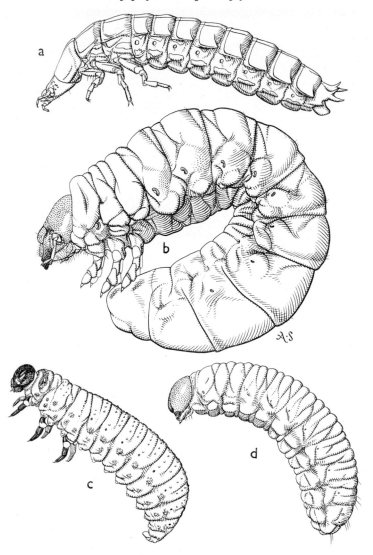

Fig. 12. Four principal types of larval insects: *a, campodeiform*, active, often carnivorous; *b,* s*carabaeiform*, generally living in the soil, decaying vegetation, at the roots of plants, and so on; *c, eruciform*, caterpillar-like, often browsing on the leaves of plants; *d, apodous*, or completely legless type, living among abundant food

Plate 22. A clothes-moth, Order Lepidoptera, with scaly wings

there is no clear rule as to which insects need most. Generally all insects of one species have the same number of instars, but even this can vary, especially under bad living conditions.

There is not much to say about *nymphs*, except in the aquatic groups like mayflies (EPHEMEROPTERA) and dragonflies (ODONATA). Here the problems of living under water have been met by a number of special structures such as the *gills* of various kinds (figs. 8, 9), which we have discussed earlier in this chapter.

Larvae, on the other hand, have an enormous range of shape and size. Those of parasitic insects hatch from the egg to find themselves surrounded by unlimited food, and need only the simplest kind of organs to feed upon it. Indeed in such a situation there is no need for the egg to have a large store of food as yolk, and the larvae, in effect, hatches prematurely while still an embryo.

The larvae of other holometabolous insects fall into two general groups: those with legs, and those without. This is not quite as casual a distinction as it might seem. The possession of legs is related to the activity of the larva, and this again to its feeding habits. Very active, quick-running larvae, like those of many beetles, may have three pairs of well-developed segmented legs on the thorax, but no abdominal appendages, except at the tip (fig. 12a): these are known as *campodeiform* larvae, because they look like the genus *Campodea* of the Class

Plate 23. A hawk-moth, Order Lepidoptera

DIPLURA. The fat, grub-like beetle larvae that are found in soil, decaying wood, dead leaves, and so on, are called *scarabeiform*, because the well-known chafers (Scarabeidae) have larvae of this type. These again, have three pairs of legs on the thorax, and non on the abdomen (fig. 12b).

These two types of larvae are called *oligopod* (i.e. 'few legs'). *Polypod* larvae (i.e. 'with many legs'), in addition to the segmented legs of the thorax, also have false legs (*prolegs*, or *pseudopods*) on some at least of the abdominal segments. Caterpillars (also called *eruciform* larvae, fig. 12c) are polypod larvae, and are found in butterflies and moths (LEPIDOPTERA), scorpion flies (MECOPTERA) andsaw flies (HYMEN-OPTERA-Symphyta). The prolegs are rather shapeless swellings, which in Lepidoptera, but not in sawflies, are equipped with tiny hooks (*crochets*).

Larvae that have no legs at all (*apodous*, fig. 12d) generally live among a mass of food-material. Though legless, they are not necessarily immobile; maggots of flies, for example, can move quickly and purposefully by wriggling, and sometimes by jumping (see Chapter V). They are always evolved from ancestors that did have legs, and distinct vestiges of these may sometimes be visible. Apodous larvae are found in several families of beetles; among bees and wasps where the parent insects provide food for the larvae, and in all groups of flies and fleas.

When an insect starts life as one type of larva, and later changes to a different type, with different feeding habits, this is called *hypermeta-morphosis*.

PUPAE

The larvae of holometabolous insects are so different from the adults—and what is more, they make no progress towards adult structure during the successive larval instars—that when the time comes to metamorphose into an adult a complete reconstruction is needed. This can be carried out only during a resting stage, when all normal activities except respiration cease.

This stage is called the *pupa*, from the Latin for a female infant or a doll. It looks rather like a modern sculpture, with the head, thorax and abdomen, antennae, legs and wings, all present in the rough, but lacking in detail, and held in a stiff, unnatural attitude (fig. 2). Since this is a vulnerable stage it is often protected by an outer casing. The mature larva may build a case just before pupation, either by spinning silk into a *cocoon*, or by shaping earth or wood fragments into a *pupal cell*. In the more advanced groups of flies (DIPTERA), such as the blowflies and allied families, the skin of the last larval instar is hardened into a seed-like casing called a *puparium*.

The pupa itself is always enveloped in its own cuticle or skin, whether or not it is further enclosed in a cocoon or puparium. If the pupal skin is arranged in such a way that the appendages are free to move, the pupa is said to be *exarate*, or 'free'; if the appendages are swaddled down to the body the pupa is *obtect*.

Pupae of both types normally remain still, or at any rate, inactive. Many insects have a period of activity just before they emerge as adults, but this is now considered to be a distinct stage of metamorphosis, during which the insect is adult, but is still confined within the pupal skin. It is then called a *pharate adult*. It is the pharate adult that often climbs out of the water or soil, so that the adult can emerge in the open air.

IV. HOW THEY BECOME AWARE OF THEIR SURROUNDINGS

(*Sight; hearing; touch; smell and taste*)

We take our own senses for granted, and look on things as being 'real' only if we can see, hear, touch, smell or taste them. We know that other people's senses never work in exactly the same way as our own: some persons can hear the high-pitched sounds of bats or grasshoppers, to which others are quite deaf; and we have only to consider the selection of clothes worn by some people, to realise that their perception of colour must differ widely from our own. Nevertheless, we instinctively trust our own senses as a guide to what the world around us is really like, and it is extremely difficult to put ourselves into the place of an animal so far removed from us as an insect.

If we stand in a sunny garden and watch bees flying in and out of a hive, it is natural to think that they can see the garden as we see it; that they pick out a promising blossom and fly to it in a purposeful way. It needs an effort of will to put the human viewpoint out of mind, and to enquire exactly how much the bee really knows of what is going on round about.

Let us look first at the senses of an insect, which give it messages from the outside world, and then, in the next two chapters, let us see how an insect may respond to these messages.

Sight

The whole body surface of insects seems to be sensitive to light to some extent, and those insects that live in caves and similar dark places may be able to distinguish light from darkness, even though they have no eyes.

Normal sight in insects, however, depends on special organs, which are of two kinds, *compound eyes* and *simple eyes*.

Compound eyes are the principal organ of sight, the 'eyes' proper, of adult insects. The outer surface of each eye consists of a number of *facets*, varying from one in some insects to over 20,000 in others. If there are only a few facets these remain circular, but in most insects the facets are tightly packed together, and are hexagonal, as in a honeycomb (Plates 51, 52).

Each facet is in fact the end of a tubular structure called an *ommatidium*, so that a section through the eye, shown diagrammatically, looks like fig. 13. A single ommatidium has something of the same structure as a human eye, but its working is quite different. The human eye works like a camera. The cornea and lens together throw an image on the retina, as if on the film in a camera, and objects at varying distances are brought into sharp focus by muscular control of the lens. In the insect's ommatidium the facet and the crystalline cone beneath it are like the cornea and lens of the human eye, and produce an image which falls on a retina at the further end of the tube; but there the resemblance ends. The insect's eye has no means of focusing, and the retina of one ommatidium cannot register anything more than an impression of a spot of light.

The effect of all the ommatidia together is to produce a mosaic of spots of light, each of a brightness corresponding with that of the part of the field of view that is in line with that particular tube. In this way

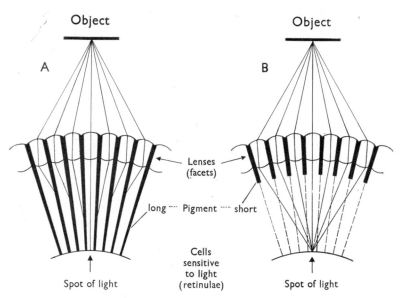

Fig. 13. Diagram of part of a compound eye of an insect: A, 'day-adapted', with each component (ommatidium) separated from the others by pigment, so that the point on the retina, marked by the arrow, receives light from one facet only; B, 'night-adapted', with the pigment drawn back, so that each point on the retina receives light from a number of adjacent facets

the compound eye produces a picture of the scene in front of it, very much like a photograph as reproduced in a newspaper or book by the half-tone process.

That such a mosaic is produced in fact, and not just in theory, was shown by a German, Exner, seventy years ago, who actually took a photograph through the eye of an insect; so did Eltringham in England, forty years later.

The tubular part of an ommatidium is called a *lens-cylinder*, and normally its sides are black for at least part of their length. If the lens-cylinder is entirely black (fig. 13A), and each ommatidium is therefore a dark tube cut off from the others, then the spots of light in the compound image are clear and distinct. This gives a picture of maximum definition, like a picture printed on good quality book-paper, through a fine half-tone screen. This is generally what happens in day-flying insects, when the light intensity is ample.

Night-flying insects often have the lens-cylinders longer, and without pigment for much of their length. This allows the light coming straight down one cylinder to be reinforced by rays coming in through the sides from adjacent facets (fig. 13B). Thus the spots of light in the compound image are made brighter, but of course correspondingly more blurred.

In many insects the pigment on the walls of the lens-cylinders moves

Plate 24. A silk-moth, Order Lepidoptera

61

in response to light-intensity. Thus in a strong light we have the cylinder-walls black, and the picture at its sharpest; in a weak light the pigment retreats and allows the more blurred, night-adapted image to be formed.

A mosaic image of this kind gives an insect only an imperfect picture of what lies before it. That is why it is a mistake to think of insects as moving about in a world of solid objects such as we ourselves see. Their view must be rather like that we have through the frosted glass of the bathroom window, but without our advantage of knowing what it looks like with the window open. Insects obviously can distinguish shapes to some extent, and the bees and wasps can find their way back to their hive or nest again. But *movement* is the thing that really attracts their attention. A robberfly lives by chasing flying insects and catching them in the air, but it will equally well follow a piece of thistledown, or a tiny paper ball.

It has always been a puzzle why the lens-cylinder should be so long, why a simple spot could not be produced nearer to the surface of the eye. Recent work of great precision, with minute electrodes inserted at various points along the cylinder, has shown a sequence of *diffraction images*, each in succession with greater resolution, able to detect smaller and smaller movements of the test object. This important discovery shows that the length of the lens-cylinder is essential to its operation. It also shows that one ommatidium alone can detect movement.

A single compound eye can give little idea of distance, except what can be inferred from the size of the object seen: i.e. the number of facets of the eye that it occupies. In most insects the space immediately ahead comes into the field of view of both compound eyes, and this gives a sort of rangefinding device, rather like our own stereoscopic vision, except that the insect's eyes are fixed, and cannot squint like ours. Predaceous insects seem to be able to wait patiently until their prey is just at the right distance before snapping at it.

The question of *colour* sense is too complicated to discuss here. It is certain that many insects can distinguish some colours, though probably never quite the same spectrum that we can see. When making experiments it is difficult to make sure that the insect is really distinguishing between two colours, and is not being guided instead by shape, or differences in light intensity; just as colour-blind people generally behave quite normally, even though they may live in an all-grey world, or one in which all greens are bright red.

Ocelli are simple eyes, with only a single facet, though they often occur in groups of three or six. They are of two kinds, the *dorsal ocelli* of adult insects, and the *lateral ocelli* of larvae.

Dorsal ocelli are to be found at the top of the head, or *vertex*. Three is the full number, though there is some evidence that the middle, or median ocellus is a double structure. Sometimes only the median ocellus is present; sometimes only the two lateral ones; in a great many insects the ocelli are completely absent. It is believed that the ancestral insects had ocelli, and that where they are now absent they have been lost in the course of evolution.

The dorsal ocelli have something of the structure of an eye, but they do not seem to be good enough to produce any sort of detailed picture. They are believed to record the general light intensity, and to be more sensitive to fluctuations in light intensity than are the compound eyes. It has been suggested that they may help flying insects to keep their balance in the air, but a great many flying insects do quite well without them; moreover they may be present in one genus of insects, and absent in a close relative. The most likely function of dorsal ocelli is that when stimulated by light they may 'tone up' the insect's nervous system, and put it on the alert.

Lateral ocelli (*stemmata*) occur on the sides of head of larvae of many Orders. They have the same 'toning up' function as the dorsal ocelli, and in addition they seem to give some larvae a rough idea of nearby objects. Where there is a group of six ocelli on each side of the head, as in caterpillars of Lepidoptera, they may combine to form a rudimentary eye, but this is much less effective than the compound eye of an adult insect.

Hearing

Hearing is not a commonplace activity among insects, as it is with us, nor is it certain that all insects can hear. On the contrary, it seems likely that most insects live in a soundless world, and that those that have developed hearing as a special sense use it mainly to solve the problem of how to find the other sex for mating purposes.

Even among insects that show any response to sound, only a minority have special organs for it. Most make use of the hairs of the surface of the body, which may be set vibrating by sound-waves, thus exciting the nerves of the hair-socket. This is really only a special development of the sense of touch, mentioned later in this chapter (fig. 14a).

Caterpillars can 'hear' in this way with the hairs all over the body, and will show that they hear by stopping movement, and 'freezing'. In ants, and especially in male mosquitoes, it is the hairs of the antennae that are specially developed for this purpose. The hairs of caterpillars are said to respond to notes ranging from three octaves below middle C to two octaves above this, but as the response to the high notes is not synchronous—i.e. the hair vibrates irregularly, or jarringly, and not in tune with the sound—it does not seem that the insect can listen to such sounds in any discriminating way.

Moreover, if these high notes are so badly received, it means that the higher overtones of ordinary sounds will be distorted, and reception will be far from being 'hi-fi'. In all, therefore, it seems that the musical response of the hairs of an insect is an incidental and unimportant sideline to their real purpose of being delicate organs of touch.

Certain special organs of hearing in insects are called *tympanal* organs, because they have a tympanum, or drum, of thin skin, connected with a group of special cells called *chordotonal sensillae*. The latter involve a nerve-cell and several other cells, drawn out into a fibre-like structure, which is stretched between a fixed point on the body and a movable

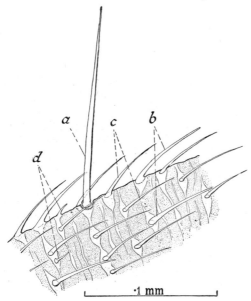

Fig. 14. Surface view of an antennal segment, to show various sensory hairs: *a*, a spine sensitive to touch; *b*, thin-walled hairs (sensillae) believed to react to smell or taste; *c*, *d*, thick-walled hairs, perhaps reacting to changes of temperature. From Wigglesworth, 1953.

one, such as the base of a hair, or the drum of the tympanal organ. These sensillae respond to any change of tension—i.e. slight tightening or slackening—by generating nerve-currents. Chordotonal sensillae are not specially organs of hearing, but are found all over the body of an insect, and are used to register any kind of movement or a force of any nature; a sort of internal stress-gauge. This is particularly true of *Johnston's Organ*, a structure found in the second segment of the antennae of many insects (e.g. mosquitoes), where sensillae of this type res-

Plate 25. The caterpillar of a geometrid moth, Order Lepidoptera, is called a 'looper', because its false legs are near the tip of the abdomen, which is strongly arched upwards as the caterpillar crawls

A Shell Photograph

pond to any vibration of the long 'flagellum' of the antenna. Not only does this organ help males to find females by hearing their flight-tone; it also registers airflow over the head and is used in flight control.

There is little logic about which insects should have tympanal organs, and whereabouts on the body they are placed. The short-horned grasshoppers have them on the first segment of the abdomen. but the long-horned grasshoppers and crickets have them on the forelegs. Many bugs and moths have them in the thorax, but cicadas and some moths have them in the abdomen; no butterflies have them at all.

Like the hairs, the tympanal organs respond to sound, but it is not certain that this is their true purpose. There is still the problem of what sounds they are meant to receive, and whether other insects of the same group can make such sounds.

The insect's voice is very poor compared with our own. We use our breath to vibrate a pair of vocal chords, and by varying the tension of the chords and the resonance of our throat, nose and mouth we have a tremendous range of pitch and timbre. Apart from the buzz, hum or whine produced by the vibration of its wings, an insect generally can make only sounds of a scraping or scratching kind, by rubbing together two parts of its body. This is called *stridulation*, and although in principle it is akin to musical instruments of the violin family, the crude construction and small size of the insect's apparatus makes the refined and subtle tone of the violin quite beyond its powers.

Stridulation is particularly associated with the grasshoppers and their allies, where nearly always it is the male that makes the sound. Stridulation may result from rubbing together specially roughened areas of the wings, or by rubbing a leg against a wing. The sound is different in different groups, and varies from a dry crackling to a high pitched-noise like the 'singing' of a tea-kettle. Among the common grasshoppers of an English meadow there are differences of song, which have been studied by means of tape recordings. Besides the differences of pitch and quality that arise from variations in size and structure between different species, there are also differences of rhythm. One entomologist claimed to be able to distinguish between two species of grasshopper in the field by watching the movements of the legs through field-glasses.

The chirping of the cricket on the hearth suggests a Victorian cosiness, though nowadays we should be more likely to send for the Public Health Inspector. Like their allies, the long-horned grasshoppers, crickets do not use the legs when stridulating, but rub the right hind-wing against the left, when specially roughened, file-like veins produce the piercing chirp.

Stridulating Orthoptera are good ventriloquists, and cicadas (Hemi-

Plate 26. A 'woolly bear', the caterpillar of a tiger-moth, Order Lepidoptera, is protected from its enemies by long, irritating hairs

Plate 27. The caterpillars of the clothes-moth, Order Lepidoptera, normally live a concealed life, and are bare and unprotected. Here they are shown exposed on a piece of material

Plate 29. At the other extreme of the Order Diptera is this warble-fly, stout and hairy

contact with the sense organ. Whether fine droplets suspended in the air are smelled or tasted is a matter of opinion.

For these olfactory senses, the insect has no special organ to correspond to our nose or tongue, but again makes use of a number of tiny mechanisms scattered over the surface of the body. These are further modifications of those very versatile sensory hairs that have already been used for detecting sounds and for giving the sensation of touch. The cuticle has become so thin that the molecules of the chemical to be detected can pass through it, and stimulate a bundle of nerve-endings below.

Sometimes the area of thin cuticle is still visible as a hair: sometimes this hair is recessed in a pit, or in a bulb at the end of a long stalk; sometimes there is merely a flat area (*pore-plate*) on the surface of the body (figs. 14, 15). Olfactory hairs are mainly found on the legs (tarsi) and on the proboscis; olfactory pits on the palpi and antennae; and pore-plates on the antennae.

Imms (1957, p. 96) lists four principal ways in which the sense of smell is used by insects.

1. *Sexual attraction.* The 'assembling' of male moths to a virgin female moth is a well-known phenomenon. The males show the same reaction to certain pure chemicals, though there is as yet no evidence that female moths actually produce these particular chemicals.

2. *Recognition odours.* Ants and bees can recognise the odour of

Plate 30. The larvae of the culicine mosquitoes, Order Diptera, hang from the surface of the water as they breathe through their siphons

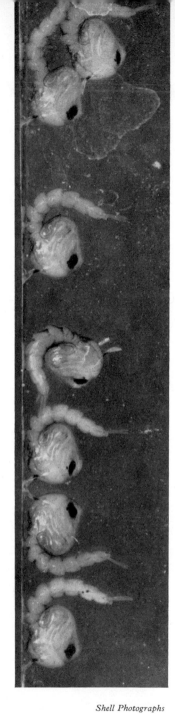

Plate 31. The pupae of the same mosquito have their breathing-spiracles on the thorax

Shell Photographs

Plate 32. This bee-fly, Order Diptera, feeds from primroses in the spring

their own species: ants follow trails laid down by other ants, and are temporarily confused if you rub a finger across the trail; bees recognise and fight invaders from other nests. It has been suggested that the reason why hibernating flies come into the same house year after year may be that the swarms leave an odour behind them.

3. *Oviposition attractants.* It is well known that a great many insects are attracted by smell to a place suitable for egg-laying: e.g. blowflies to meat. Here again there is the fact that pure chemical odours attract insects even though these substances do not occur naturally: e.g. sea-weed flies are irresistibly attracted by trichloroethylene which, though somewhat related chemically to the halogen compounds in sea-weed, is not a natural odour.

4. *Food attractants.* Very similar to oviposition attractants, and in some cases—e.g. dung insects—it may be difficult to say which is the more important basis of attraction.

The sense of *taste* in insects has been studied by offering them substances that taste sweet, sour, salt or bitter to us, and seeing their reactions. In this way it is possible to tell which substances they are able to distinguish from each other, and whether they like them or not. Honey-bees are specially suitable for this kind of experiment, because they are domesticated insects, and a great deal is already known about their way of life. As might be expected, bees are particularly discriminating in their tasting of sweet substances, and will reject not only artificial sweeteners such as saccharin, but also many true sugars that seem reasonably sweet to the human palate.

The chief organ of taste is the mouth, but insects may also have taste-cells in the antennae and in the tarsi of the legs. These organs are used to make a preliminary inspection of their surroundings, and many insects will at once extend their proboscis if their tarsi come in contact with a sugar solution.

V. HOW INSECTS MOVE

(Crawling; walking and running; jumping; swimming; flight)

Muscular movement

Since insects have an external skeleton, made up of plates of hardened skin, all the muscles have to be accommodated inside this. There is therefore a network of muscles criss-crossing from one plate, or sclerite, to another, to control all the possible movements at the various joints. This is especially so in the thorax, which is almost entirely filled with the muscles needed to operate the six legs and one or two pairs of wings. The muscles may be attached to the inner surface of a sclerite, or to an internal ridge called a *phragma* or an *apodeme*.

If a muscle is attached to a phragma, or to a small sclerite, or to the inside of a tubular sclerite, such as a segment of a leg, then it has a rigid attachment against which to pull. The bigger, flatter sclerites of the thorax and abdomen have a certain flexibility, and may be distorted when a muscle pulls them. This, which might seem to be a defect, is used to advantage in two of the most important muscular activities of insects. We have already seen how compression of the abdominal segments helps to force air in and out of the body during breathing; below, under the heading of flight, we shall see how distortion of the thorax by two opposing sets of muscles operates the wings.

The ways in which insects move from one place to another may be classified as follows:

Crawling

When we think of 'crawling' we think of moving along on the belly, as opposed to being supported by legs. Except for a few degenerate forms, which do not move, the nymphs of Hemimetabolous insects and the adults of nearly all groups have thoracic legs, and either walk or run; crawling is mainly an activity of the larvae of Holometabola. Many of these have thoracic legs, but those larvae in which the abdomen rests on the ground have to progress by a crawling motion, helped sometimes by the fleshy pseudopods, or prolegs that are often found on some of the abdominal segments.

Crawling is most highly developed in caterpillars, which have a

74

cylindrical abdomen clearly divided into segments, each of which has horizontal and vertical muscles. Several of the segments have fleshy prolegs, which in Lepidoptera are equipped with hooks or *crochets* to help them to grip.

By pulling alternately on the upper (dorsal) and lower (ventral) horizontal muscles, and with suitably timed contractions of the vertical muscles, each pair of prolegs is lifted up, moved forward, and planted down again (fig. 61). The abdomen is thus moved forward with that rippling movement that we have all seen caterpillars make. The 'looper' caterpillars of the family Geometridae generally have prolegs only on the sixth and tenth abdominal segments (Plate 25), and so the second pair have to reach a long way forward at each step. This causes the body of the caterpillar to be arched upwards into the 'loop' that gives them their name.

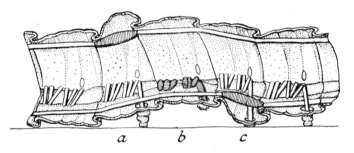

a   b   c

Fig. 16. Diagram of the action of the muscles when a caterpillar is crawling towards the right: in segment *a* the upper, or dorsal longitudinal muscles have contracted; in segment *b* the vertical (dorso-ventral) muscles have contracted, raising the false leg from the ground; in segment *c* the lower, or ventral longitudinal muscles have contracted, pulling segment *b* forward. From Wigglesworth, 1953

Larvae of flies (maggots and grubs) have a rather similar way of crawling, but their pseudopods extend in a ring all round each segment, and the larva can wriggle in any direction, not merely up and down. They also make use of their mouth-hooks to grip and pull themselves along (see also below, under 'jumping').

Just before the emergence of an adult insect of the Holometabola from its pupa, the latter generally works its way up to the surface of soil or wood in which it has been buried, by similar crawling movements of the abdomen. Instead of prolegs, the pupa often has rows of backwardly

Plate 33. A hover-fly, Order Diptera

projecting spines which grip surrounding surfaces. When the insect is clear of obstructions the skin splits and the adult emerges. It is present practice to reserve the term 'pupa' for the quiescent stage during which the larva is being remodelled into an adult, and to say that the active movements we have just described are really made by the adult still in its pupal skin. It is then called a 'pharate adult'.

Walking, Running and Jumping

Four-legged animals have two quite different ways of moving their legs. A horse when walking or trotting moves the near fore-, off hind-, near hind- and off fore-legs, in the familiar clip-clopping rhythm. This is clearly based on a twisting movement of the body, the fore-quarters twisting to the right while the hind-quarters twist to the left. On the other hand, when a horse gallops it changes to an up-and-down bending of the spine, with the two hind-legs moving together.

Insects likewise have two types of motion rather similar to these, except that the movement is largely confined to the legs, and does not twist the body so much. The first movement is rather more complicated when there are three pairs of legs to manage. In principle, the fore and hind near legs go forward, together with the off middle, while the insect remains balanced on a tripod formed from the other three legs; then

76

Plate 34. A magnificent robber-fly, Order Diptera, with a wing-span of more than two inches

the first set give support while the other three move. Since the thorax does not twist, the effect is to swing the whole body from side to side, and the insect moves with a seaman-like roll. Studying the legs by slow-motion film shows that, like the legs of horses, they do not move exactly together, but have an off-beat rhythm.

The insect uses this first type of motion at all speeds, and does not change abruptly, as a horse does when it begins to canter. The hind-legs are used together, however, in *jumping*, and may be powerfully developed for this purpose, as in grasshoppers and fleas (fig. 1; Plate 38). Other insects jump strongly without using their legs.

'Springtails' (Collembola) have a special two-pronged organ, called a *furcula*, attached to the fourth abdominal segment, and extending forwards under the abdomen, where its tip is held by a catch (*retinaculum*). When the furcula is released it presses down on the surface beneath the insect, and throws the springtail up and forward, just like those jumping frogs that children have.

'Click-beetles' (Frontispiece: family Elateridae, the larvae of which are 'wireworms') have a jumping mechanism of a rather different kind. Underneath the thorax a stiff projection from the prothorax presses against the edge of a pit in the mesothorax. When it slips over the rim the thorax is given a violent twitch, in a sort of tiddleywink action. This mechanism is used when the insect falls over on to its back, and the

77

effect is to throw the beetle into the air, when it has a chance of alighting on its feet.

Swimming

Some aquatic insects move only on the surface of the water, some move with their bodies almost, but not quite submerged, and the majority live below the surface, entirely surrounded by water.

The first group are the 'skaters', and are supported by the *surface-tension* of the water (fig. 5). To break through the surface of water requires a definite force, the amount of which is in proportion to the area to be broken. If an object is placed on the surface its weight tends to drag it down, and the surface tension to support it. Weight depends on volume, surface tension on area. Since a small object has a surface area large in proportion to its weight, some insects are able to walk on the water without breaking through. Those which practice this often increase the effect of surface tension still more by covering the body with fine hairs, or branching filaments, and by making the body surface oily or waxy so that it is difficult to wet.

The skaters are carnivorous bugs of the Hemiptera-Heteroptera. The water-measurers (Hydrometridae) are stick-like insects with long legs, and crawl about on the water just as if they were on dry land. By contrast, the true pond-skaters (Gerridae) use the two middle legs together, in a leaping, or rowing movement, steering with the trailing hind-legs.

The whirligig beetles (fig. 17a), which live on the surface with only their backs exposed, propel themselves by using the submerged legs like oars. The middle- and hind-legs are broader than usual, and grip the water well; the fore-legs are used for seizing the prey on which this carnivorous insect feeds.

The underwater swimmers—water boatmen (fig. 17e), back-swimmers and water-beetles—also use the hind-legs as oars, moving them together in the second, or jumping movement, not alternately as in running on land. These limbs, and sometimes the middle pair as well, are broader than usual and have fringes of long hairs. In action, they are turned edge-wise on the forward stroke, just as an oar is feathered.

All these insects take a supply of air down with them as a bubble. The water-scorpions (Nepidae) on the other hand, stay within reach of the surface with their long siphon, and simply walk about on the submerged plants, as if they were on land: they have no special modifications, except for hydrostatic organs which warn them before they go too deep for their siphon to operate.

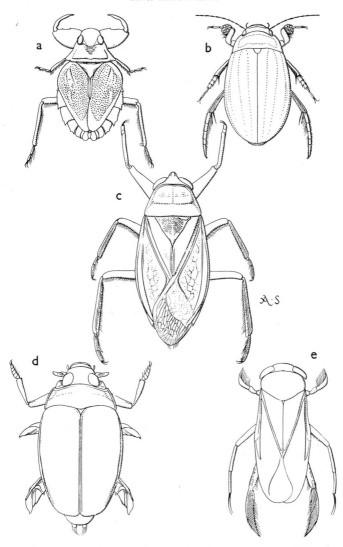

Fig. 17. Some water-bugs and water-beetles: *a*, a naucorid bug, which creeps about on submerged vegetation, and has powerful grasping fore-legs; *b*, a dytiscid beetle; *c*, a giant water-bug; *d*, a whirligig beetle, which darts about on the surface; *e*, a water-boatman, a corixid bug that is a very capable swimmer. Notice the various modifications of the legs for swimming and for seizing prey

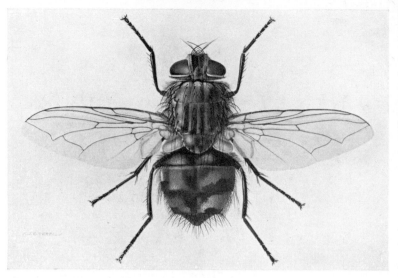

Plate 35. The common bluebottle, Order Diptera, shown here in a drawing
by Terzi, has a neat array of thoracic bristles

As on land, larval insects in the water make use of the abdomen,
wriggling to propel themselves along. This is seen most strikingly in
the larva of the fly, *Chaoborus*, often called *Corethra*, which seems to
have two silvery spots in its body. These air-sacs are connected with
the tracheal system, and by varying the volume of these the buoyancy
of the body can be controlled. It is a mistake to say, as some textbooks
do, that by this means the larva can maintain itself at any desired level.
Water is practically incompressible, and so its density does not vary
much at moderate depths. The density of the water does, however, vary
with temperature, and with mineral content. What the air-sacs do is to
adjust the buoyancy until the *Chaoborus* larva is only just a little denser
than the water round about. If the larva remains still it will sink slowly,
but by twitching the body it can quickly rise to any desired level, and
from there float slowly down again.

Flight

Three living groups of animals are able to fly: birds, bats and insects.
Flying-fishes have wing-like fins, but use them mainly as gliding-
planes. Even if they may stretch the glide by flapping the fins once or

Plate 36. A flesh-fly, Order Diptera

twice, this does not compare with the controlled, purposeful flight of the other three groups.

The earliest insects were without wings, and some of the existing groups evidently branched off from the main evolutionary stem in this early wingless period. These are the Sub-class Apterygota (see Chapter I). All other insects have winged ancestors, even though some of their modern representatives may have lost their wings again.

The construction of the wings has been discussed in Chapter II: here we are concerned with how they are used in flight. The wings beat with an up-and-down movement, combined with a twisting at the base, which serves both to drive the insect through the air, and to steer it. What the wing-beat does, in effect, is to bring about a reduction of air-pressure above the insect—which balances its weight—and to one side. or the other—which causes the insect to move bodily in that direction

In most insects the up-and-down beat of the wings is produced by the *indirect* wing-muscles. The wing is pivoted on the side-plate (*pleuron*) of the thorax, and its base attached to the dorsal plate (*tergum*). When the horizontal muscles cause the tergum to bulge upwards this forces the wing-tip down; when the vertical muscles pull the tergum back again, the wings are raised.

81

Plate 37. An acalyptrate fly, Order Diptera

The twisting of the wing is caused by *direct* muscles, which are attached to one or other of the *axillary sclerites*, little hard pieces fixed in the base of the wing. The principal *veins*, or stiffening ribs of the wing arise from these sclerites, and the action of the direct flight muscles twists the wing by acting on these veins.

It will be noted that none of the flight muscles is actually inside the structure of the wing, which is entirely operated by forces acting on the extreme base of the veins, a remarkable mechanical feat.

There is nearly always a tendency for the veins of the wing to be thicker and closer together towards the leading edge of the wing giving this additional stiffness, as in an aircraft wing. The trailing edge of an aircraft wing is thin, and mainly composed of hinged portions, flaps and ailerons, which are used to control speed and stability in flight. The trailing edge of an insect's wing is similarly divided into lobes, the shape and flexibility of which varies enormously in different insects (cf. Plates 15–20). The remarkable thing about the insect's wing is that these lobes of the flexible trailing edge are not under muscular control, but bend automatically as the wing moves, and their efficiency in action is a matter of design, not of operation.

The direct and indirect muscles are not independent of each other, because the side-wall of the thorax is not a rigid fulcrum. Although strengthened internally, the pleura have some elasticity, and consequently the effect of both indirect and direct wing muscles is more complex than the simple picture given above. It is analysed in detail by Pringle (1957), and, with remarkable use of photography, by Nachtigall (1972).

The *frequency of wing-beat* varies from 4 per second in some butterflies to about 1000 per second in a tiny midge. Insects with a slow wingbeat produce each muscular contraction by a single nerve impulse. This allows them to control each wing separately, but it quickly becomes impossible at higher frequencies, since the chemical link between nerve and muscle cannot work quickly enough. A fascinating example of the efficiency of design—that is achieved by the processes of evolution was revealed by the discovery that insects with high frequencies of wingbeat had indirect muscles of a very special kind, known as fibrillar muscle, which contracts if it is suddenly stretched, and relaxes if it is released. Put two sets of opposing muscles of this material in an elastic box such as the thorax of an insect, and a single nerve impulse will be followed by a stream of rapid contractions of the two sets alternately. The frequency of muscular action depends on the natural rhythm of the thorax, and the nerve impulses now serve only to excite the muscle into activity.

With this mechanism flies and bees and similar insects have a powerplant that works at its own built-in speed, leaving the direct wingmuscles to twist the wings independently, and thus direct all this power into vertical lift, or into horizontal movement, or any combination of the two. It is this combination of power from the indirect muscles and control from the direct muscles that gives hovering insects their astonishing powers of manoeuvre in the air.

Like most other structures, the wings have tended to become simpler during evolution. No insect is ever known to have had three pairs of wings, and most insects find two pairs difficult to manage without some modification. The smaller dragonflies (damselflies), and the scorpionflies (Mecoptera) have the two pairs of wings almost identical. They fly well, but rather slowly, with a twinkling motion of the delicate wings, more like helicopters than true aeroplanes. The two pairs of wings do not beat strictly together: the hind pair is usually ahead on the down-beat with the result, that it gets a grip on the air before it is disturbed by the fore-wing.

Insects that use their wings in a businesslike way, to get them quickly from place to place, seem to have found it necessary to do one of two things: either to lock together the two wings on each side so that they function as one; or to use one pair of wings to do most of the work of flying, and either reduce the others to a small size, or to adapt them for some other purpose.

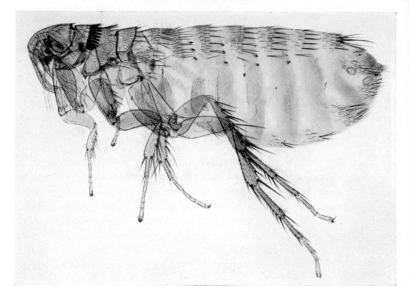

Plate 38. A flea, Order Siphonaptera. This species is found on the wood-mouse

This process has started in grasshoppers, where the fore-wing is narrower and more leathery than the hind one. It still beats like a wing, but at rest it forms a cover, hiding the bright colour of the hind-wing and camouflaging the insect. The hind-wing, on the other hand, is elaborately folded like a fan. Beetles have gone further, with the fore-wings hardened into stiff, horny *elytra*, which are held up at an angle during flight. They do not beat, and their function is more that of fixed aerofoil surfaces like the wings of an aeroplane. The hind-wings of beetles, in contrast, have an exceptionally broad sweep, and may move through nearly 180°, from straight up to straight down.

In the Hemiptera-Homoptera (plant-lice and related forms) the fore-wings are narrower and tougher than the hind pair, and in the Hemiptera-Heteroptera they are divided into a stiff part and a membranous part, from which the name Hemiptera, or 'half-wings' is derived. On the other hand, according to Pringle (1957), Hemiptera tend to rely for flight mainly on the fore-wings, and 'even a cicada can fly satisfactorily without the hind-wings'.

Another solution, that of locking the wings of each side together, is seen in Lepidoptera (butterflies and moths), where there is a tendency for the insect to become a tiny, narrow body supported between the

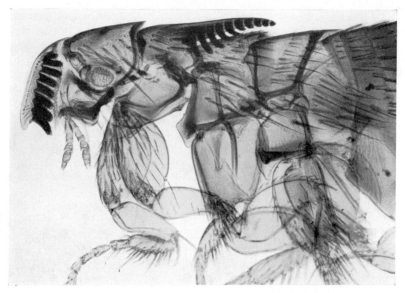

Plate 39. Head and thorax of a rat-flea from the Argentine, which has an elaborate set of combs

enormous wings. Hymenoptera have filmy, membranous wings (hence their name), which are firmly held together by the engagement of a tiny row of hooks (*hamuli*) on the hind-wing, with the trailing edge of the fore-wing. This is the final stage in making the fore- and hind-wing beat as one.

Yet another solution to the difficulties of managing two pairs of wings is to get rid of one pair altogether. Mayflies (Plate 4) have gone a long way in this direction, reducing the hind-wings to small ovals, with an area much below that of the broad fore-wings: occasionally the hind-wings have gone altogether. The true flies (DIPTERA, Plates 32–37) have converted the hind-wings into knobbed organs called *halteres*, which beat during flight, and which are believed to act like gyroscope enabling the fly to balance better, and taking over some of the functions of directional control from the wings. The fact that flies are among the most efficient performers in the air suggests that it is better to have one really good pair of wings than to try to co-ordinate two pairs.

An aeroplane has a number of separate devices for controlling its speed, rate of ascent or descent, change of direction, and stability in the air. An insect does all these things by minute variations in the path followed by the wings in each beat.

85

The wing-tip generally follows a figure-8, or crossed loop pattern, going downwards and forwards, upwards and back. Like an oarsman, the insect squares its blade on the downward, or power stroke, and feathers it for the recovery. All the elaborate control is achieved by varying the angle of the blade, and its speed of movement, at different points of the path, and by changing the plane of the stroke on one or both sides. The most expert fliers, such as the bees and the hoverflies, have complete control in the air, and can hover motionless, rise or fall, or dart forwards, or backwards, or to either side, simply by altering the stroke-plane of the wings.

How is the insect able to make such delicate adjustments with such speed and precision? In the base of the wing there are nerves, and a number of *sensillae*, rather like those we have mentioned before in connection with hearing. These tell the insect what the wing is doing, just as we ourselves can move our hand behind our back, without being able to see it. In addition there are certain *reflexes*, or automatic actions which concern flight. If the tarsi of the legs cease to press against a solid surface most insects will begin to fly. Once the insect has begun to move through the air it seems to be aware of the flow of air over its antennae, and over certain sensitive hairs on the face. Other experiments with locusts have suggested that the apparent movement of the ground is used as a guide.

The *speed* at which insects can fly has been much exaggerated. As we have seen, the damselflies and scorpionflies flit about quite slowly, and their speed is said to be 1–3 m.p.h.—a walking pace. Bumblebees and hoverflies, though their wings move too quickly to be seen and give them the appearance of great speeds, in fact move at only about 6–10 m.p.h. Horseflies follow cars and trains at speeds up to about 25–30 m.p.h. Hocking (1953, *Trans. R. Ent. Soc. Lond.* 104; p. 302) calculates an absolute maximum speed of 36 m.p.h., and a sustained speed of not more than 24 m.p.h. for one of the biggest Australian dragonflies, and says that he doubts if any insect can go much beyond this.

The legend that a certain fly can reach 800 m.p.h. is based on an unsound observation. In 1926 an entomologist reported that he had seen botflies cover a distance of 400 yds. in one second, which worked out at 818 m.p.h. Both time and distance were estimated, without using any instruments. In later papers he claimed to have recognised the species of the fly, and its sex, and yet said that it was 'of course totally invisible at top speed', and became visible only when it slowed down to avoid him! It seems incredible that anyone ever took such a claim seriously, but instead of questioning the soundness of the original observation, people made elaborate calculations to prove or disprove that it was

Plate 40. A sawfly, Order Hymenoptera-Symphyta. Note the network of large cells in the wing, and the absence of a 'waist' to the abdomen

possible to push such a hairy insect through the air at supersonic speeds, and if it were, whether the energy necessary could be generated in so small a body.

Soaring Flight

We have already seen how insects may be supported on the surface of water, if they have a surface area that is large in proportion to their weight. A similar process occurs in the air. Very small insects fall through the air extremely slowly, because they generate so much frictional air resistance in proportion to their weight. This is true if they are very soft-bodied and light in weight, like the aphids (greenfly); or have hairy wings which enormously increase the air-resistance, like the thrips (Order Thysanoptera); or are exceedingly minute, like many parasitic Hymenoptera: the fairy-flies (Mymaridae), parasitic in eggs of other insects, may be less than one-quarter of a millimetre long.

Once these insects have taken wing they are like a feeble swimmer in a strong current, and are carried away bodily, not only horizontally with the wind, but vertically by convection currents and atmospheric turbulence. If you watch a patch of brilliant sunlight, either in a wood, where shafts of light fall across a dark background, or towards evening, when the rays are more horizontal, you can see the spots of light glinting from these insects as they are carried to and fro in the air. They obviously have little power of controlled flight compared with, say, a wasp or a bee.

It is mostly these insects that are carried up in the air to great heights, and from one continent to another, across oceans and deserts. Now and then good fliers, such as hoverflies, have alighted on ships far out to sea and have obviously been carried away by the wind from their usual haunts, and have gone on flying mechanically until they found somewhere to alight. Quite large butterflies and other insects take part in mass migrations, as we shall see in the next chapter. But by and large, the insects that are carried helplessly from one country to another are the small and the weak fliers, and it is from these that much of the insect population of remote areas has been derived.

VI. HOW INSECTS BEHAVE

*(Reflexes; instincts; swarming; migration; insect communities;
social insects; signs of intelligence)*

We have seen how the various senses of insects tell them about their surroundings, and how the insects themselves can move in various ways. Behaviour is the way in which an insect reacts to a particular situation, by receiving impressions from its various senses, and then responding with an appropriate set of movements.

Reflexes

The simplest item of behaviour is a *reflex action*, in which one sense organ is linked by nerves directly to a muscle. Fig. 18 shows such a *reflex arc*, passing through one of the nervous junctions, or *ganglia* of the central nervous system. An example of a reflex has been mentioned earlier: when an insect's weight ceases to press on the tarsi of the legs, the wings may be set in motion.

Much of an insect's behaviour is made up of simple automatic reflexes like this. So, indeed, is much of our own, as when we instantly pull our finger away from a hot plate, or blink when something comes near to our eye.

The insect's nervous system is much less concentrated than ours, and a reflex arc may be complete without going to the brain. Hence reflex movements of the legs or wings can go on for a time even after an insect has been decapitated. Nevertheless, under normal conditions, the reflexes are not entirely automatic, but may be modified or suppressed altogether in certain circumstances. For example larvae often have a reflex movement upwards and towards the light, which takes them up into the vegetation to feed; but when they are fully fed the reflexes are reversed, so that they now move downwards and away from the light, which takes them under cover on the ground, where they pupate.

Instinctive Behaviour

A reflex is a single item of behaviour; a more complicated sequence of acts that seem to follow automatically in certain circumstances is classed as instinctive behaviour.

Certain species of horsefly of the genus *Chrysops* live in the rain-

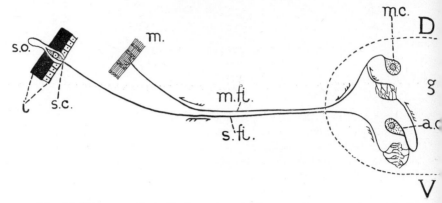

Fig. 18. Diagram of a 'reflex' arc, by which a muscle reacts automatically to a sensory stimulus: *s.o.* is the sense organ in the skin, or integument (*i*)*;* the sensory neurone (*s.c.*) sends an impulse along the sensory nerve fibre (*s. fi.*) to the association cell (*a.c.*), which passes the impulses to the motor cell (*m.c.*)*;* finally the motor nerve fibre (*m.fi.*) carries the signal to activate the muscle (*m*). From Imms, 1957

forests of Africa, and in the dense forest the larvae of the fly live in shallow streams, among mud and decaying vegetation. When the adult fly emerges from the pupa it disappears from the breeding-site, and is to be found in the high forest canopy, 80–100 ft. up in the trees. Most of the species feed there at night on monkeys, but one species feeds by day on humans moving about in clearings, near villages, and around their fires. After the fly has fed on blood its eggs ripen and, then the fly returns, not to the tree-tops, but to the stream again, to lay eggs, concealing them so well that in spite of prolonged study, only once or twice have they been found. Yet the eggs must be there, since larvae are plentiful.

Unless we are prepared to assume that the fly has an intelligent understanding of what it is trying to do, we have to believe that at different times of its adult life it is governed by quite different patterns of instinctive behaviour.

Thorpe (1948, *Bulletin of Animal Behaviour*, No. 7, p. 7) gives another example, the fly *Stomoxys ochrosoma*, also in Africa, which flies over columns of the army ant, and drops its (the fly's) larva in front of one of the worker ants that is returning empty-handed to the nest. It is believed that the ant obediently carries the larva into the nest, where it

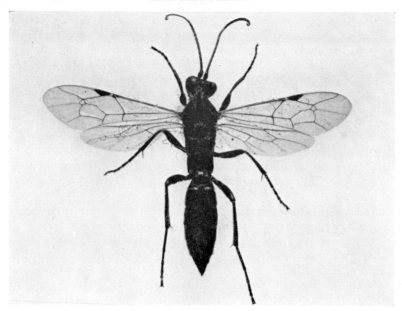

Plate 41. An ichneumon-fly. Order Hymenoptera-Parasitica

grows up. Thorpe points out that: 'It seems likely that the fly can distinguish visually between: (1) workers and soldiers; (2) "empty-handed workers" and laden ones; and possibly (3) workers travelling away from the nest and workers travelling nestwards.'

Instincts of this kind are inborn and inherited, and exist somewhere in the nervous system of the insect, all ready to be triggered off by some outside stimulus. If no opportunity occurs for the mechanism to go off normally it becomes 'trigger-happy' (or, more formally, 'the threshold of release is lowered') and the insect may go through the motions at quite the wrong time. In this, after all, it is only like a small child at a school concert, who laboriously learns a part, and then, impatient of waiting, goes through his act from the wrong cue.

Instinctive behaviour in insects can be modified by training, showing that insects are not at the mercy of entirely automatic, mechanical behaviour. A single example is the way in which bee-keepers persuade a colony of bees to move from one hive to another, or even combine two colonies in one hive. To avoid strife among the bees, the move is made by a succession of small changes, allowing time for the bees to become accustomed to each one before making the next move.

Swarming

Insects, like people, are gregarious at times, and seem to feel an urge to congregate among others of their kind. This is a kind of reflex response. When the temperature falls, the adults of a number of species of insect have an impulse to move away from the light, and to press themselves against some other object. This leads them to hibernate in dark corners, all closely packed together, sometimes in thousands. Many attics and lofts have such a swarm of hibernating flies during the winter months.

Three kinds of swarms are familiar to most people: swarms of bees; swarms of midges on summer evenings; and the destructive swarms of locusts.

Swarms of bees are part of the elaborate social life of bees, to which we shall come later in this chapter.

Swarms of midges are one among many instances of insects which congregate in the air for mating purposes. The swarm is normally composed of males, and as it rises and falls in the breeze it is conspicuous to us, and presumably to females of its own species. These fly in, mate and fly out again. It seems that the swarm is a convenient way of bringing the sexes together, and shortening the time that they might otherwise have to spend in searching for each other. This is particularly important among insects that breed in water and have only a short adult life in the air—e.g. mayflies—and in those like the winter-gnats (Trichoceridae), whose aerial activity is limited to the few hours of a winter's day when the temperature is high enough for them to fly.

Swarms of locusts have been studied a great deal, because they do so much damage to crops whenever they settle. Uvarov (1921, *Bulletin of Entomological Research*, No. 12, p. 135) first explained this behaviour by the *Phase Theory*. For a number of generations locusts behave like ordinary grasshoppers, feeding in certain of the swampy grasslands of the Middle East: this is the *solitary phase*. After a period of rapidly increasing numbers, there comes a change both of appearance and behaviour, as they enter the *gregarious phase*. They now become excited by the closeness of other individuals, and the population finally moves off as a body across hundreds of miles of country, to new breeding grounds.

Locusts are bred in England regularly for experimental purposes, and they can be caused to develop into the solitary or the gregarious phase at will by varying the conditions under which they live, particularly the extent to which they are crowded together. The phases are different, not only in behaviour, but in colour and shape. The solitary grasshopper is light green, the gregarious locust yellowish brown.

Migration

It is only a step from the swarming of locusts to the migration of insects. In fact, Williams (1958, *Insect Migration*), who has dealt exhaustively with this subject from a lifetime of experience, points out that some other migratory insects, notably moths, have two phases, a dark swarming one and a pale solitary one. Yet he is careful to emphasise that apparently insects do not migrate just because they are overcrowded.

The Monarch butterfly in North America is the best known insect migrant. During the summer the butterflies are not crowded together, but are scattered over the countryside, in the way that butterflies usually are. Yet at the end of summer they assemble, and move southwards in great numbers, covering perhaps a thousand miles. When they settle down for the winter they are strongly gregarious, and pack themselves tightly together, several thousand per tree. In the spring the butterflies wake up, and fly back northwards one at a time, not as a band.

This butterfly illustrates several characteristics of insect migration. Breeding takes place at the more northerly (i.e. colder) end of the range, and the movement south avoids the rigours of the winter. The stay at the southern end is merely a resting stage. It is significant that the butterflies assemble together for the southern journey but make the return individually. Because of this it used to be thought that mass flights of insects took place in one direction only, and if this had been so it could not have been called migration in the true sense of the word. It seemed then to be a way of shedding surplus population, and it was difficult to explain how such a habit could have arisen in evolution.

Now, however, it seems likely that every mass flight has its return movement, though the returning insects, being scattered, are more difficult to observe. Williams lists some thirty different species of butterfly that are known to migrate and return. Some of them, like the Monarch, breed at one end of the range and rest at the other; some breed at both ends of the range (like the locusts) and arrive there at the most favourable season. Migrating insects other than butterflies include dragonflies and hoverflies.

Williams gives a whole chapter to discussing what might decide the direction of flight, We must distinguish between the *course*, which is the direction in which the insect points its head and tries to move, and the *track*, which is the direction in which it actually moves over the ground, under the combined influence of its own flight and the effect of the wind. As insects rise higher above the ground the wind velocity generally becomes greater; when it becomes greater than the maximum speed at which the insects can fly, then they are carried steadily downwind regardless of their own efforts. This has been particularly observed in locusts.

Some insects, notably bees, ants and beetles, have been shown to be able to steer a course by the sun, the so-called 'light-compass reaction'. The Robinson Light Trap is based upon a similar reaction in moths and other night-flying insects. The insect tries to keep the point of light on the same facets of the eye all the time. If the source of light is far away, e.g. the sun or the moon, then the insect continues in a straight line, keeping a constant angle to the beam of light. When the light comes from a lamp not far away, the only way to keep a constant angle to the beam is to turn steadily towards the lamp in a spiral path, which eventually brings the insect into the trap.

Difficulties arise when this theory is applied to migrating insects, which continue in the same direction for days, or even weeks. Williams points out that they would have to make a continuous correction for the apparent movement of the sun through the day, and moreover they are able to carry on just the same on a dull day, or a moonless night, or after they have been interrupted by bad weather.

Certain insects, notably migratory aphids, seem to need a period of active flight before they can settle down and reproduce, but in general 'we know neither the external cause not the internal mechanism' of the

Plate 42. A solitary wasp, Order Hymenoptera-Aculeata

migration of insects (Williams, 1958). Although we know that a strong wind may override the orientation of the migrating insects—i.e. the direction in which they are facing and trying to move—this does not explain the orientation but relegates it to a secondary importance.

Johnson (1960) suggests a general tendency for all insects to make an 'exodus flight' from their breeding site as soon as they are hardened enough to do so. This is seen as an individual reaction, but when many individuals emerge at the same time it becomes a mass migration.

Insect Communities

It is not easy to draw a line between a swarm and a community, but one might say that a swarm is essentially a temporary gathering for some particular purpose (mating; hibernation), whereas a community is a more lasting association.

One of the best known of insect communities is one of aphids (greenfly) on a garden plant (Plates 13, 14). Here can often be found all stages of one or more generations living close together, feeding, reproducing, growing up. Such an assembly probably came about in a negative way, in the sense that the insects concerned are peaceful plant-feeders, surrounded by an abundance of food, and so there is no reason why they should disperse. Those which thus spend their whole lives

Plate 43. A solitary bee, Order Hymenoptera-Aculeata

Plate 44. A wingless mutillid wasp,
Order Hymenoptera-Aculeata

on a single plant derive the biological advantage they that do not have
to search for the other sex, nor for a suitable place in which to lay eggs.

Greenfly are able, in a few weeks of summer, to build up very large
populations, using sedentary wingless females that reproduce partheno-
genetically, that is without the intervention of males. Winged females
appear from time to time, especially if living conditions become
unfavourable, and then fly to other plants, where fresh colonies are
established. In autumn there appear males and egg-laying females. The
over-wintering eggs are usually laid on the twigs of woody plants, where
the young larvae emerging in the spring can feed on the opening buds.
Insects tend to gather in communities wherever an abundance of
food brings them together. 'Plagues' of caterpillars are an example of
how the coincidence of several favourable factors can bring about a
sudden increase of population. One factor is the weather, particularly
that of the preceding winter. Over-wintering insects are biologically
adjusted to tolerate a certain amount of cold, and even of frost, and often
cannot develop properly without a resting-period, or *diapause*, in cold
weather. A mild, open winter keeps them too active, uses up their store
of energy-giving food too soon, and exposes them to the attacks of birds.
On the other hand, a late, cold spring means delay in starting the season
of growth and reproduction. In most years one factor will be favourable,
others not; but occasionally there is a year in which all the factors are
in the insect's favour, and a big population is the result.

An early season is most helpful to insects that have several generations during the summer. If the population increases fourfold at each generation, then a season that permits one extra generation to be fitted in will give a final population four times as big as usual. This may account for certain years in which there are outbreaks of seaweed flies, or of the little yellow-and-black swarming fly, *Thaumatomyia notata*, in houses.

Some insects live in communities of more modest size, which remain the same, without great seasonal fluctuations in numbers. These often occur where the breeding habits of the insects restrict them to situations that are limited in extent. Fleas, for example, breed in debris round the living- or sleeping-quarters of the animal host. The larvae of the fleas feed on scraps from the skin of the host, and mainly on the droppings of the adult fleas, which contain undigested blood. Consequently fleas are parasites of animals (mammals and birds) that have a den or nest, and they live in a community there with the adult fleas riding about on the host animal, but coming back frequently to the community-site.

Ant-lions (Order Neuroptera, family Myrmeleontidae, Plate 16) have a fiercely carnivorous larva which lives at the bottom of a conical pit in fine sand or dust (Wheeler called them 'Demons of the Dust'). Here they lie concealed until some insect wanders on to the steep slope of the pit and beings to slither down it. When the ant-lion hears—or feels the vibration of—the grains of sand dislodged and falling down, it helps the process by jerking its head and throwing sand at the prey until it falls to the bottom, when it is seized and eaten.

Plate 45. An exceptionally large chalcid, Hymenoptera-Parasitica

The community of ant-lions comes into being because only a few places are suitable for the pits. The sand or dust must be very fine, and quite dry, and the place must be sheltered from rain, otherwise the first shower would obliterate the pits and drown the larvae. Suitable places are in the entrances of dry caves, under overhanging rocks and on the verandahs of native huts that have an earthen floor. The community is a drawback to the individuals, since the prey has to be shared among so many, and sometimes the pits are so close together that it is surprising that any ants fall into them at all.

Ant-lions are found only in warmer countries, but a similar kind of community can be seen in sandy areas in Britain. The burrows of solitary bees and wasps are made in earth or soft sand, and are often bunched together in communities for the same reasons as the pits of the ant-lions, because suitable sites are limited in extent.

A spectacular insect community is that of the *New Zealand Glow-Worm* (Plates 57, 58). This is not a true glow-worm (which is a beetle), but is a small fly, *Arachnocampa luminosa*, of the family Mycetophilidae. The larvae lives in communities in caves, surrounded by hanging threads covered with a sticky material. The larvae are luminous, and attract small insects, which are then trapped and devoured. In this instance community life is beneficial to the individuals, because the combined pattern of large numbers of larvae and filaments makes a better light-trap for insects than a single larva could.

Social Insects

It is again a short step from living in a community of independent individuals to living in a society, in which the individuals are dependent on each other. The simplest social life is maternal care of the young, and signs of this can be seen in some insects which congregate for egg-laying, and afterwards brood their eggs.

The female of the horse-fly, *Goniops chrysocoma*, lays its eggs on a leaf over water, and attaches itself to the leaf by means of its claws. In this position it remains until the eggs are hatched, and ultimately dies, still attached to the leaf. Rhagionid flies of the genus *Atherix* also assemble in this way over their egg-batches on a leaf. The clusters of the females of *Atherix ibis* that are occasionally found in Britain look like swarms of bees.

It used to be thought that as soon as the young larvae of *Atherix* had hatched from the egg they fell into the water and lived independent lives. Recent work has shown that in some species at least the tiny first stage larva remains on the leaf and moults before taking to the water, so that we have the rudiments of maternal care.

Plate 46. A ground-beetle, Order Coleoptera, damaging a strawberry
A Shell Photograph

Care of the young to this stage, or beyond, is shown also by earwigs and by certain plant-bugs.

The more advanced forms of social life are found in two Orders of insects, Isoptera (termites) and Hymenoptera (bees, wasps, ants). These two Orders are only distantly related in other ways, and their social behaviour has been developed quite independently. It is all the more remarkable that they have reached so many similarities, as a result of *convergence*, of which we shall have more to say in the following chapter. There still remain profound differences between the two insect 'civilisations'.

Let us consider first what features of social life the two Orders have in common. They live in large colonies, with hundreds of thousands of individuals, and they share the work of the nest by a division of labour based on a system of *castes* (Plate 7). Egg-laying is confined to fertile females known as *queens*, of which there are few, or even only one per nest. Fertile males are also few, and almost all the members of the nest are sexually sterile, occupied exclusively with foraging for food, nest-building, looking after young larvae or defending the nest against attack.

Which caste an individual belongs to is decided partly by whether it developed from a fertilised egg or not, and partly by the food it receives during its larval life. Once it has become adult it does not change caste. Members of different castes are different in appearance as well as in behaviour.

The chief difference between the social life of the two Orders is that in the termites, the workers and soldiers may be sterile individuals of either sex, whereas the workers of the social Hymenoptera are all sterile females. In the Hymenoptera the males exist only for the nuptial flight, and afterwards die or are killed off before the winter. In the termites one male remains fertile in the nest, and periodically re-fertilises the female.

ISOPTERA—*Termites*

The termites, the destructive 'white ants' of the tropics, fall into two biological groups. The dry-wood termites burrow in wood above ground level, and often cause wooden structures to collapse suddenly without warning. The subterranean termites nest in the ground, but go on extending the nest above ground level to produce the termitaria, or 'ant-hills' that are such a feature of tropical scenery. Some of the biggest termitaria are to be seen in Australia, and may be 12–20 ft. high, and 10 ft. in diameter. Inside they are a sponge-like mass of connecting spaces, but the structure is of a very unsponge-like hardness, which sometimes can be broken up only by explosives.

The nuptial flight of termites involves fully winged males and females, which are produced in a nest or colony at intervals and, issue in a swarm. Many are killed by birds or lizards, but the few that survive cast their wings and go off in pairs to found a nest. Mating does not take place in the air, but in a nuptial chamber that the insects construct either in wood or in the ground.

The eggs laid by the queen give rise to sterile males and females, which act as workers to feed the colony, and soldiers to guard it. There are a number of different forms of these, to which names are given. As time goes on the abdomen of the queen becomes distended, the membrane being stretched, and the abdominal plates widely separated (Plate 9), until the queen becomes a mere bag of eggs, with a small head and thorax attached. A mature queen of some groups may lay several thousand eggs a day, being fertilised at intervals by her consort male, and storing the sperm in her spermatheca.

At long intervals fertile males and females, with wings ('alate reproductives') are produced and swarm out of the nest, to pair off and found new colonies. It is believed that the royal pair can live over a long period of years, and if one of them dies, then a replacement, or supplementary reproductive, makes its appearance.

The termites are more difficult to study than the Hymenoptera, or at any rate than the bees, and it is not known exactly how the workers are able to produce fertile males and females in place of sterile ones. By analogy with bees it is thought that changing the diet may be the explanation.

Termites are among the few insects that can digest cellulose, and so are able to feed on the plant-tissue itself, and not only on its sugary and starchy contents. That is why they are able to live on dead wood and be so destructive to it. The digestion of the cellulose is in fact carried out by single-celled animals called Protozoa, which live in the intestine of the termite and pass on to it the chemical products of the breakdown of the wood.

Besides cellulose, termites eat other plant material, lichens and fungi. Columns of workers come out at night, protected by soldiers, to collect suitable food material and take it back to the nest. In addition, some groups cultivate 'fungus-gardens' inside the nest, where they grow their own food.

There is a good deal of passing on of food from one individual to another, either from the mouth, mixed with saliva, or as faecal droppings. The latter is the means by which the intestinal Protozoa are passed

G

Plate 47. The larva of a ground-beetle is carnivorous and beneficial
A Shell Photograph

on to other individuals. This resembles the mutual exchange of food in nests of Hymenoptera, which Wheeler called 'trophallaxis'.

Social HYMENOPTERA — *wasps, bees, ants*

Wasps and bees exist at all levels, from a solitary life to the most highly organised social life in a nest, but the truly social species are very much in the minority. In Britain, out of nearly 250 species of bees, fewer than 30 are social, and of nearly 300 species of wasps, fewer than 10.

WASPS

Adult wasps live on sugary foods—how they can ruin a tree of ripe fruit—but their larvae are carnivorous, and have to be supplied with animal food. The solitary wasps (Plate 42) either make burrows in sandy soil, or build earthen cells attached to twigs. In suitable patches of sand the burrows of 'fossorial' wasps (and bees) may be congregated together, but this is a community like that of the ant-lions, we have mentioned above, and not a social group.

The adult wasp provisions its nursery cell by catching an insect and stinging it until it is immobilised, though not killed. The family Sphegidae burrow in the ground and use a single caterpillar to feed their young. The Pompilidae catch a spider and also put it into a burrow in the soil. The Crabronidae catch flies and pack them away in large numbers, either in the ground or in rotting woodwork: it is startling to find that a window-frame or a doorpost is rotten inside, and tenanted by a mixed lot of wasps and flies.

When the food is provided and an egg is laid, the cell is usually sealed off and left to look after itself. Some wasps, however, continue to supply food after the larva has hatched, and this is possibly a hint as to how maternal care and true social life may have evolved.

The true social wasps are the familiar yellow-and-black wasps of our garden, the Hornet, and one or two related, but less well-known species. The fertilised females, or queen wasps, spend the winter in sheltered places, and can be seen on warm spring days, restlessly searching for a suitable nesting place. They choose a hollow of some kind in the, ground, or in the roof of a porch or outhouse, and there build a comb of cells from 'wasp-paper'—a sort of papier-mâché made from wood chewed with saliva.

The larvae that hatch from the eggs are fed with portions of other insects, previously chewed up by the adult wasp. At first the queen feeds her brood, but the adult wasps that develop from it are sterile females and take on the duties of workers. They now do all the cell-building and foraging, and leave the queen to concentrate on laying more and more eggs.

The wasps that are a nuisance in the fruit and jam season are workers, and can both bite and sting. They sting to paralyse their insect prey, and bite to feed themselves with fruit or other sugary foods, to masticate food for their larvae, and to scrape off fragments of wood to build cells in their comb.

Later in the summer bigger cells are built, and in these fertile females and fertile males are reared. The sterility of the workers is a result of insufficient, or incomplete feeding of the larvae, and fertile females can be produced by improving the diet. The males develop from unfertilised eggs. As we have seen, the female parent receives sperm from the male and stores it in a receptacle called a spermatheca, from which the eggs are fertilised before they are laid. Towards autumn eggs begin to be laid without having been fertilised.

After the mating flight, the males and the workers all die, and only the fertilised queens survive to start new nests in the following year.

BEES

Like the wasps, the bees are mainly solitary, but they also demonstrate various intermediate steps towards the full social life of the honey-bee.

Bees are not carnivorous. They have mandibles, which are sometimes well developed, as in the leaf-cutter bees, but the principal feature of the mouthparts is a 'tongue' formed from the very much lengthened glossae of the labium (fig. 10e). Flowers conceal a store of nectar, a sugary solution, which the bees collect and keep for a while in their crop, where it undergoes chemical action, and is transformed into honey. The honey is later brought up again and stored in the cells of the hive.

Besides the nectar, a flower exposes pollen on its stamens in such a position that the bee brushes against it when it takes the nectar. As the bee goes from flower to flower it transfers pollen from one blossom to another, and so ensures cross-pollination. At the same time the bee generally collects the pollen that sticks to its hairy coat, and carries it in special pollen-baskets, usually on the hind-legs, but sometimes underneath the abdomen. If you watch a bee visiting flowers you will see these yellow masses of pollen, often absurdly big for the size of the insect.

Like the solitary wasps, the solitary bees (Plate 43) live in holes in soil or sand, or in burrows in decaying stumps and posts, and congregate in suitable places to give a community of colony of individuals living close together, but not taking part in a true social life. They provision their cells then lay an egg and close the cell, leaving the larva to fend for

Plate 48. The clover-seed weevil, Order Coleoptera

A Shell Photograph

itself when it hatches. The leaf-cutting bees (*Megachile*) cut out neat pieces from the leaves of roses and other garden plants, and use them to line their cells inside burrows in rotting posts. The mason-bees (*Osmia*) build cells of a salivary cement containing fragments of wood, sand or soil, and put them in odd cavities and crevices, including key-holes.

Everyone knows the *bumblebees*, of which there are nearly twenty different species in Britain. They have reached the same level as the social wasps, and their life-story is similar. The fertilised queens hibernate and appear in spring to make a nest. This is in some existing hollow, especially the empty nest of a field mouse or vole, where on a layer of moss or leaves the bee makes a waxen cell, provisioning it with pollen and honey, and laying several eggs in it. She looks after the larvae that emerge, and gives them more food when they need it. Sterile female workers gradually take over the duties of foraging and cell-building, and the queen finally does nothing but lay eggs. In late summer fertile females and males appear, and after mating only the fertilised females survive the winter, to begin new colonies in the spring.

The most completely social life among bees is that of the honey-bee, *Apis mellifera*, which is now almost entirely a domesticated species, but which is believed to be descended from a wild ancestor in the East. A colony may contain more than 50,000 bees, and may go on from year to year indefinitely.

Like the other bees, and the wasps, a honey-bee colony is dominated by a *queen*, and there are two other castes, *workers* and males (or *drones*). All the workers are sterile females, and the only function of the drones is to take part in a mating-flight, when the queen is fertilised once for her lifetime.

The workers build and maintain a comb of hexagonal cells, some of which are used for breeding purposes, and some as stores of honey for winter food. The comb is of wax, which the young workers produce from glands in the abdomen. The queen lays one egg in each cell of the brood comb, and when the larvae hatch they are fed by workers. Carbohydrates are supplied in the form of honey and pollen, and proteins in the form of 'royal jelly', which comes from glands in the mouth of the workers.

Males (drones) develop from unfertilised eggs, which the queen is able to lay by omitting to expose them to sperm from the spermatheca. These eggs are laid in special drone-cells, which are bigger than the average. Eggs that have been fertilised always develop into female bees, but whether these bees themselves remain sterile and become workers, or attain full sexual development and become queens, is determined by the diet upon which the larvae are reared. Nearly all the larvae are fed mainly on honey and pollen, and on this diet they remain sterile, and become workers. From time to time the workers construct queen-cells, much bigger than the rest, and hanging down from the comb, and the larvae in these are fed entirely on royal jelly.

When the hive becomes overcrowded, the queen leads a *swarm* of workers to found a new hive at another site. The workers that are left behind rear another virgin queen, which goes out on a mating flight with the drones, and then returns to take over the job of egg-laying in the nest.

The life of the honey-bee has been studied in greater detail than that of any other insect, and is mentioned by classical authors, and in the Bible. People have always been fascinated by the problem of how the bees find their way about. Not only do the workers forage for a mile or so round the hive, and return confidently to it, but they are apparently able to pass on information to the other bees inside. As soon as the forager has found a crop that is in flower, and has returned to the hive, other bees come out and fly to the same flowers.

Ingenious theories have been put forward by von Frisch and others to explain how this is done by performing a 'dance' on the comb, among the other workers. The path followed by the bee during its dance, and the orientation of this path on the comb, together with the timing of the dance, and the spacing of certain pauses for a shaking of the abdomen, are said to tell the other bees how far off is the source of nectar, and in what direction. The experiments on which this is based are described in detail by Ribbands (1953, *Behaviour and Social Life of Honey-Bees*).

They may be summarised by saying that the bee returning from having found a source of nectar is supposed to note its direction from the sun and the distance back to the hive, and then to translate these from a horizontal plane into a complicated symbolic dance on a vertical comb. The other bees are supposed to appreciate this dance, in the dark, and when they come out into the bright light, to be able to interpret it back on to a horizontal plane, and in the reverse direction. Incredulity is answered by the fact that they do get there, and if not by this means, how else?

ANTS

There are no solitary ants. All ants live in social colonies that are permanent, and both colonies and the individual ants in them may survive for many years.

Like the bees and wasps, the queen ants are fertilised in a nuptial flight, but the nuptial flights of ants take place simultaneously over a

Plate 49. Larva of an asparagus-beetle, Order Coleoptera

A Shell Photograph

wide area. It is not known just what sets them off, but it is a most remarkable phenomenon that a district will be filled with 'flying ants' on one particularly sultry summer's afternoon.

After mating, the queen ant lands and breaks off her wings, then either goes into an existing colony of ants, or starts a new one. Then, as in the wasps or the bumblebees, she lays eggs that hatch into workers, and form the nucleus of a new colony.

Most ants do little nest building, and do not make combs, but live in a labyrinth of communicating galleries in the soil, as we find when we try to destroy a nest underneath a brick path. Instead of providing each egg with a cell in which it can grow up as larva, and then as pupa, ants keep the eggs, larvae and pupae separately, and often move them about. If you break open an ant's nest you will see the workers seize all the immature insects in the damaged parts and carry them quickly away.

Only males and queens have wings and then only for the brief nuptial flight. The workers, which again are sterile females, do all their foraging on foot, running quickly about, and touching things with their long antennae. The antennae have a bend in the middle, like an elbow, and this is one of the distinguishing marks of an ant. If you watch one running along it continually waves its antennae, and often taps them against the ground, or against stones and sticks in its path: or if it does not actually touch objects it 'explores' them by bringing its antennae near. It is using its highly developed sense of smell, which we have seen in Chapter IV operates through sense organs in the antennae and the legs.

The sense of ants are very highly developed. It has been shown that as they go off on a foraging trip they keep track of their direction from the nest by noting the direction of the sun, or if the sun is not visible, they use the polarised light that comes from the sky. This is the so-called 'light-compass' reaction, which we have mentioned before, and which we shall come again to at the end of the chapter.

After a single ant has found food and returned to the nest the other workers follow the same route. It is annoying to find one of these ant-trails leading under the back door and into the larder, but the behaviour of the ants is fascinating to watch. The trail usually keeps along the bottom of the walls, and winds round corner after corner, till it finally leads up on to the shelf or table where the food is to be found. Ants scurry along it in both directions, following the scent left by the others. If you draw your finger across the trail the ants are baffled for a time, and stop in a bewildered way when they come to the invisible barrier of a strange scent: then some individuals find their way across or round the patch, and set up a new scent trail for the others to follow.

If social life in insects is measured by the extent to which individuals depend on each other, and exchange food material among themselves, then ants have the highest level of all. All kinds of food, animal and vegetable, are acceptable to them—another reason why they are at once so successful as insects and so troublesome to man. The workers give the larvae food, partly masticated and predigested: the larvae produce drops of saliva and other fluids which the workers like, and for which they continually lick and caress the larvae. The workers also obtain *honey-dew* from aphids by caressing them with their antennae, and some ants keep and tend colonies of aphids as if they were herds of cattle, for the sake of their honey-dew. When it is considered that some of the bigger ants also keep ants of a smaller species as slaves, and make them do the heavy work of the nest, it seems that their societies have almost reached the human level.

Some ants can sting, but they are best known for their powerful bite. Though the bite of one ant may be trivial to larger animals, the attack of hundreds of ants at once can be most unpleasant, and may be dangerous. In the tropics the driver ants (Dorylinae) are nomadic, and move about in dense columns, sometimes hundreds of yards long. As they pass, they destroy all the insects and small mammals they meet, and even the larger domestic animals may be killed if they are penned, and cannot escape.

Signs of Intelligence in Insects

It is hard to say what is a sign of intelligence. Our own lives are controlled by automatic, or reflex actions to a much greater extent than we often imagine. Those of us who travel over the same route every day come to make the whole journey in a mechanical fashion, not far removed from the behaviour of an ant. Which of us has never been halfway home before remembering that today he was to have done something different: or been embarrassed because when he was checked at some unexpected barrier he mechanically offered his season ticket?

A great many experiments have been made with the object of breaking down the behaviour of insects into a chain of reflex actions. We have mentioned the 'light-compass reaction' already. The basic experiment is said to show that an ant which is walking steadily in a straight line can be picked up and put down somewhere else, and will go forward in a direction parallel to the first: therefore it was not going towards a destination in a conscious way, but is moving in a line that makes a constant angle with the sun. If the insect is covered up for a few hours and then released it continues to make the same angle with the sun, even though the sunlight now comes from a different direction.

Plate 50. Eggs of the asparagus-beetle are attached to stems and petals

A Shell Photograph

Experiments like this, though interesting in themselves, raise as many problems as they solve. How does the insect get started on such a path; what makes it choose that particular angle and what makes it eventually decide to do something else? Furthermore, how does it make the return journey, and, as Williams asks, how do migrating insects maintain a true direction in spite of the apparent movement of the sun?

We ourselves do something rather like this when we walk through a dense wood, or over an open space with no landmarks. Try crossing the top of the Pennines over a peat moss, without a compass, and you will find that you are dependent on a very primitive 'sense of direction' not far removed from a 'light compass-reaction'. It might be said that anyone getting himself into such a situation was not being very intelligent, but it would not be safe to say that he had no intelligence at all.

It seems, therefore, that the elaborate experiments that have been done on the behaviour of bees and ants do not in themselves prove that these insects have no intelligence. In fact the complicated code that the dance of the bees is said to represent is so involved that it would seem that only the highest intelligence could be expected to be able to operate it, with sufficient accuracy. It would need less intelligence for the bee to go out and look for food itself.

The main reason for thinking that insects cannot have much true intelligence is the fact that their nervous system is so much smaller than our own, and apparently so much simpler. Intelligent behaviour would seem to need more nerves and nerve-junctions than they have, so that memories and impressions of past events could be stored away, and brought out on the right occasions to influence future behaviour.

Nevertheless the behaviour of insects, particularly of social insects, covers many actions that we ourselves would perform deliberately, with a conscious purpose in mind. There is even one wasp (*Sphex*) that is said to pick up a stone and use it to ram down the covering of its burrow, and thus takes its place alongside primitive man as a user of tools.

It remains to be seen whether we shall have to give the insects credit for more intelligence than we thought, or whether we shall have to look upon more of our own behaviour as being instinctive rather than purposeful.

VII. THE DIVERSITY OF INSECTS

(*Adaptation; convergence; mimicry*)

Naturalists have always marvelled at the diversity of animal life, and in particular at the way in which so many animals are beautifully constructed for the life they lead.

When it was suggested that the species as we now know them had arisen by evolution from simpler forms, it was necessary to provide some explanation of how they could have become so closely adapted to their way of life. The two principal theories were the Inheritance of Acquired Characters—generally associated with the name of Lamarck—and Natural Selection, the theory of Darwin and Wallace. These theories are discussed in the Museum booklet on *Evolution*, to which the reader is referred.

Whatever the theory, it is a fact that animals, including insects, tend all the time to grow more 'specialised', i.e. to say, more closely *adapted* to a particular mode of life. If a species is distributed over a wide area, with different conditions in different parts, then this process of specialisation is inclined to produce a number of local forms, each suited to local conditions, and slightly different from the others. Eventually these forms grow so far apart they that cease to interbreed, and become distinct species, which are said to *radiate* from a common ancestor, or stem form.

Since animals in the course of evolution become adapted to their way of life, distantly related animals often come to look superficially alike, as a result of living in the same way. This is called *convergence*. Finally, it sometimes appears that one species gets an advantage from looking like another, a phenomenon known as *mimicry*.

Adaptation

There is space to mention only a few examples of adaptation in insects. We have already (Chapter III) spoken of the mouthparts (fig. 10), which in a cockroach or a grasshopper are 'primitive', or 'generalised', and have three pairs of general-purpose organs: mandibles, maxillae and labium, the last consisting of a pair of appendages merged together. Bugs, butterflies and many flies have one pair of more of these drawn out into a tongue-like proboscis, with which they suck up liquid foods.

113

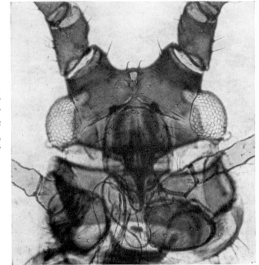

Plate 51. Head of an aphid, Order Hemiptera-Homoptera, showing the compound eyes, small, yet consisting of many hexagonal facets

Beetles, on the other hand, all bite and chew their food, and have kept the primitive kind of mouthparts.

Legs, again, are used by insects for a variety of purposes, and have been developed in a number of different ways. In their simplest form they are used for walking and running, and the femora, tibiae, and segments of the tarsi are slender, without any peculiar spines or swellings. Insects that dig in the ground often have the fore-legs shorter, broader and stronger, as in some ground beetles (Carabidae), chafers (Scarabaeidae) and dor beetles (Geotrupidae). Such adaptations are usually on the fore-legs only, and these do the work of digging while the insect is supported on the other two pairs. The fore-legs of the mole cricket (*Gryllotalpa*, Plate 2) are an extreme development.

Predatory insects, which catch other insects as food, also generally use the fore-legs for this purpose. The Order Hemiptera includes several families of predatory bugs, which may have the fore-legs specially developed for seizing and holding the prey. Fig. 17a shows some of these, which must be a fearsome instrument against a smaller insect. The best known 'raptorial fore-legs' of this kind are those of the praying mantids (Plate 1). Robberflies (Asilidae) catch their prey in flight, but generally have all three pairs of legs strong and hairy. In the air the legs hang down like a spiny basket, which envelops the prey so that it cannot escape (Plates 34, 54).

114

If the hind-legs are specially adapted, this is most often for the purpose of jumping or swimming. The grasshoppers and crickets exemplify the one, and the water-bugs and water-beetles the other (figs. 1, 17).

The appendages of the eighth and ninth segments of the abdomen in female insects combine to form the ovipositor, or egg-laying tube. The structure of the ovipositor is closely adapted to the egg-laying habits of the insect, and has been discussed in some detail in Chapter III.

Apart from these adaptations that have a direct, mechanical use, many insects have adapted their shape and colour to the needs of defence. The stick-insects and the leaf-insects (Phasmida) and some caterpillars (Plate 25) are an obvious example. The stick-insects have simply evolved a long and cylindrical shape for every part of the body, with the result that when they sit motionless among twigs they escape the notice of their enemies. Leaf-insects and leaf-butterflies (Plate 53) have gone further, and have the legs, abdomen and fore-wings flattened and coloured, like leaves: sometimes the resemblance is uncanny, with dark patches which give the impression of holes in the leaf, spots of fungus, or bird-droppings.

Adaptations to a particular way of life are common among immature insects, and especially among aquatic nymphs and larvae. We have

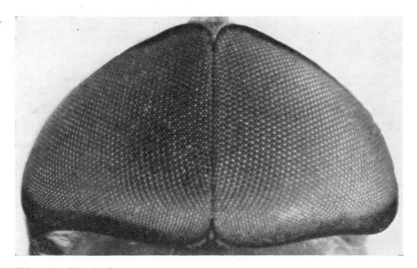

Plate 52. Head of a male horse-fly, Order Diptera, from above, showing how the huge compound eyes are so big that they meet in the middle

115

already mentioned some of these in Chapter III. Mayflies (Ephemeroptera) have a series of leaf-like or blade-like gills along each side of the abdomen. Stoneflies (Plecoptera) and alderflies (Megaloptera) have gills in the form of segmented appendages fringed on both sides. The dragonflies (Odonata), on the other hand, have two methods: either internal gills in the rectal chamber of the intestine, or three external gills at the tail.

The nymphs of dragonflies have another strongly adaptive feature in the *mask*, a double-jointed labium that can be shot forward to seize another small animal, and feed upon it.

The bodily shape, and the arrangement of the legs of larvae is, of course, closely adapted to their habits. The very active larvae, such as those of beetles (fig. 12a) have three pairs of thoracid legs, and usually lift the abdomen clear of the surface. This type of larva is generally carnivorous. Larvae like caterpillars (fig. 12e), which have prolegs on the abdomen as well as the segmented legs on the thorax, can progress only slowly, since they have to make muscular movements in the abdomen as well as in the thorax (see Chapter V). Caterpillars browse on leaves, and move steadily about, like a herd of cattle in a meadow; they do not run. Legless larvae live where food is abundant, and easily obtained, but they can move quickly to get out of a place that does not suit them. We have seen in Chapter V how they may rely on their prolegs to get them away.

A peculiar adaptation is shown by larvae of flies of the genus *Fannia*, which breed in rotting materials rich in nitrogen. The segments of the thorax and abdomen are drawn out into fringed processes, which are believed to serve as a flotation device: they increase the surface area, and so make surface tension more effective in supporting the weight of the body. The larva has to keep its hind spiracles clear of the water in order to breathe, and it is believed that increasing the surface area in this way enables the larva to survive in cesspits and other organic liquids.

Although it often seems that a particular structure, such as the ones we have mentioned, is adapted to some obvious purpose, we must not think of insects as being always built for the job, like a carefully designed machine. Many peculiar structures that are found in insects have no obvious function.

Everybody knows the 'pincers' of earwigs, which look so big and threatening, but no one knows for certain what they are used for. Three possibilities have been suggested: they might be used for attack and defence; or to grasp the other member of a pair during copulation (they are present in both sexes, but are more strongly curved in the males);

Plate 53. A leaf-butterfly Order Lepidoptera, showing the undersides of the wings, which resemble a leaf, and are exposed whcn the butterfly is at rest

or they may be needed to fold up the hind-wings, which are elaborately pleated, like a fan.

Bugs of the family Membracidae have the prothorax enormously enlarged, often into a spiky, shield-like structure. Sometimes this may help to make the insect inconspicuous on a thorny plant, as is shown in the exhibit on *Evolution*, but it seems that many Membracids have an ornate structure rather like an Emmett creation, that serves no obvious purpose. Similarly, the huge, bulbous head of some Fulgorid bugs was at one time thought to be luminous, and gave them the name of 'lantern flies', but it now seems to be without any known function.

The stag-beetles (Lucanidae), with their big mandibles, especially in the males, and the rhinoceros beetles (Dysnastinae), with their great horns on the head of the male, seem to be handicapped with clumsy structures that serve little or no useful purpose. They bring to mind pictures of the great horned dinosaurs, which became extinct in Cretaceous times, at the end of the age of reptiles. Their appearance suggests that in insects, too, evolution is not always strictly utilitarian. Theories of evolution emphasise adaptation, and the way in which structures arise in response to a need, or in a way that gives their possessors an advantage in the struggle for existence. It seems that sometimes an evolutionary process having started in one particular direction, may continue far beyond what is needed, and produce a structure that is merely a burden to the insect.

Another peculiarity of evolution is the way in which one insect may

117

develop elaborate structures in order to do something that many other insects do by quite simple means. This particularly relates to courtship behaviour, to the structure of the genitalia, and to the so-called 'secondary sexual characters', which are limited to one sex. We have seen how the habit of gathering the males into a swarm may be a benefit to insects that have a short adult life, and it is obviously helpful if a male Empid fly offers his mate a small ball of silk to occupy her attention, so that she does not attack him during mating. It is difficult to see why so many male insects have brightly coloured patches of scales on the legs, and wave these, or their spotted wings, before the female in an elaborate courtship; the great majority of insects manage to mate quite happily without doing this. Of course the same may be said of birds, where the male of the Argus Pheasant, or the Lyre Bird has resplendent plumage and an elaborate dance, while the common sparrow breeds prolifically without any such assistance.

Convergence

Insects that live in water tend to look alike, because they all have to meet the same problems of breathing and movement, and have solved them in much the same way (fig. 17). The water-bugs that swim actively—the back-swimmers (Notonectidae), water-boatmen (Corixidae) and the giant water-bugs (Belostomatidae)—have the hind-legs fringed with hairs, and the tibiae are often broadened like an oar. The legs are flattened and fringed in a similar way in the carnivorous water-beetles of the family Dytiscidae, and to a lesser extent in the Great Silver Water Beetle, *Hydrophilus piceus*, which is a scavenger, and a less powerful swimmer than *Dytiscus*.

On the other hand, the bugs and beetles that merely crawl about on submerged vegetation, without swimming actively, have normal legs, without any special resemblance to an oar. This is true of the water scorpions (Nepidae), which are bugs, and the crawling water-beetles (Haliplidae).

Convergence is even more striking among aquatic larvae. Not only the larvae of water-beetles, but the immature stages of Ephemeroptera, Plecoptera, Odonata, Megaloptera, Trichoptera and Diptera, if they live submerged in water, have developed some kind of tracheal gills, either arranged in pairs along the sides of the abdomen, or two or three projecting from its tip.

The water scorpion, *Nepa*, reaches the air by means of a long tube at the tip of its abdomen. The larvae of the drone fly, *Eristalis*, uses for the same purpose a telescopic tube bearing the hind spiracles, though it also has rectal gills for obtaining oxygen from the water.

118

Another instance of convergence through similarity of function is the sucking proboscis of the bugs (Hemiptera) and the bloodsucking flies (Diptera) (figs. 10c, d). The ancestral insects had mouthparts of a generalised kind, i.e. with the mandibles maxillae and labium not specially adapted for a particular diet, or way of feeding. Many existing insects that bite or chew their food have the mandibles with a simple cutting edge, and the maxillae and labium as simple lobes to hold and guide the food. All the insects with chewing mouthparts have probably had them throughout their evolution, the beetles as well as the grasshoppers. On the other hand, those with mouthparts adapted for sucking fluids must have evolved them from the cutting and chewing type.

Hemiptera are the most highly evolved Order of the Sub-class Hemimetabola, and Diptera are one of the more highly evolved Orders of the Sub-class Holometabola. Their sucking mouthparts must have evolved quite independently, but by convergence they have reached a remarkably similar form and function.

Mimicry

In the examples of convergence that we have discussed, the insects concerned get no advantage from resembling each other. There are, however, striking instances where two or more unrelated insects have converged in colour and pattern until they look very much alike, and if one or all of them seem to get some advantage from the likeness we say that this is a case of mimicry.

Stinging Hymenoptera, especially wasps, are dangerous foes to other animals, which mostly leave them alone. Far from concealing themselves, the biggest wasps (the Hornet, for example) are boldly patterned and brightly coloured, often in black and yellow, or black and red. This 'warning colouration' is like the striking black-and-white pattern of the skunk, which is said to give warning to other animals to keep out of the way.

If a harmless moth, beetle or fly has a pattern that gives it only a superficial resemblance to a wasp, then it would seem likely that its enemies would be deterred, and the insect would have a better chance to survive.

This is known as *Batesian mimicry*. The mimic must live in the same area as the model, and behave in much the same way. Then it is considered that an enemy, such as a bird, or a lizard, will catch a number of the models and find that they are distasteful or dangerous. After that it will leave them alone. It will also leave alone the mimics. The mimics

119

Plate 54. Not a bee, but a robberfly, Order Diptera, which mimics a bee

must be much less numerous than the models, otherwise the enemy will find that it can eat some of them.

An example of Batesian mimicry is provided by some African robber-flies called *Hyperechia* (Plate 54). These are large, fiercely carnivorous flies, which prey upon the equally large and fierce carpenter-bees of the genus *Xylocopa*. The flies have evolved a shape and colour that is not merely like a *Xylocopa*, but which quite uncannily resembles the parti-cular species of the bee that the fly attacks. Thus protectively camou-flaged, the adult robberfly can move among the bees, to catch and kill them, and to lay its eggs near the burrow, so that its larvae can go inside and feed on the larvae of the bees.

There are several species of *Hyperechia*, each preying on a *Xylocopa*, which it closely resembles. The odds against this arising by mere chance are impossibly great, and there can be no doubt that, in this case at least, the advantage to the fly has been great enough to bring about this mimetic resemblance by natural selection. Not all mimics copy their model so well as *Hyperechia* does, but this is an exceptional case, where the fly has to deceive the model itself, and to go among the bees without their being aware of it. Most mimics do not deceive the model, but its enemies, and they do not need to be good enough to stand up to close examination. All that is necessary is that an enemy should be made to hesitate for a brief moment, during which the mimic can escape.

There is a second kind of mimicry, which is said to exist between two or more equally dangerous or unpalatable insects. As Imms puts it (1947, *Insect Natural History*, p. 204), if a species has to lose 500 individuals before its enemies learn that it is unpalatable, then it is an obvious advantage for two species to look alike, and hence to lose only 250 each. This is called *Müllerian mimicry*. Obviously both species must be unpalatable, or dangerous, and you do not have a model and a mimic as in Batesian mimicry.

As an argument, this is somewhat less convincing than the theory of Batesian mimicry, but it is an observed fact that there are certain conspicuous patterns of warning colouration that are shared by a variety of different insects.

This is not the whole of the story. When you study insects from different parts of the world you find that the insects—or at least the bigger and more showy ones—of each continent have something alike in their appearance. It is hard to say exactly what this is. Perhaps there is a tendency for many of the insects of one continent to repeat the same shades of colour, rather in the way that you recognise the work of some artists by their fondness for a particular shade of mauve, or blue-green. An experienced entomologist can often look at a box of insects and successfully guess whether they came from Africa, or South America, or the Far East, just by their general colour.

It is evident that the evolution and natural selection of shape, colour and pattern is a subtle process, which is as yet imperfectly understood.

VIII. INSECTS AND US

Entomologists are often asked: 'What good are insects?' It is disconcerting to give an enthusiastic account of the appearance or the behaviour of some exotic insect, and then to be met with a puzzled frown and the comment: 'Yes, that is remarkable, but what good does it do?'

There is no foundation for the common belief that insects must be here for some purpose. They just exist, and their existence is a challenge to us to find out more about them, in the same way that people want to climb Mount Everest 'because it is there'.

All the same, the lives of insects cross with ours at many points, and when they do so, their activities may be a help or a hindrance to us. In our self-centred way we then classify them as beneficial or harmful insects, and call them 'Insect friends and foes'.

Harmful Insects

The damage caused by insects is generally an outcome of their feeding habits. Like other groups of animals, a very large number of insects feed on plants or on vegetable juices; another large group feed upon rotting materials of either vegetable or animal origin; a third group are carnivorous, feeding upon the herbivorous insects; and a fourth group are parasites, feeding at the expense of bigger animals, which they do not normally kill, but suck their blood, or destroy their tissues.

CULTIVATED CROPS

Plant-feeding insects do a tremendous amount of damage to cultivated crops (Plates 13, 14, 46, 48, 49, 55). The principal leaf-eaters are the grasshoppers (especially the gregarious locusts), and the caterpillars of the Lepidoptera and of the sawflies (Hymenoptera). These insects have surprisingly large appetites, and they are especially destructive because they are liable suddenly to appear in very large numbers, and so to devour enough of the foliage at the same time to set back the growth of the plant, or even to kill it altogether. In Chapter VI we have seen how locusts suddenly break out in migrating swarms of millions of individuals, and can strip the vegetation in one place overnight.

Less is known about the cause of 'plagues' of caterpillars, though every gardener has experienced one at some time or other. It seems that plant-feeding insects normally have a very high rate of mortality: they lay a great many eggs, but few of the offspring survive, nearly all of them being killed by unfavourable weather, or unsuitable food, or eaten by predators.

Just now and then, however, the insect has a run of luck, and all the factors happen for a while to go in its favour. The balance between a herbivorous insect and its enemies is a complex one, and Thompson (1956, *Annual Review of Entomology*, **1**, p. 401) maintains that there is no simple sequence of cause and effect. On the contrary, with so many different factors involved the final result follows the laws of pure chance. 'The usual variation in the numerical value of field populations from year to year corresponds to curves based on numbers selected at random.'

Be that as it may, the population of any insect varies greatly from one year to another. Collectors of insects can quote examples of insects that are thought of as rare for many years, and which suddenly re-appear. For several years they flourish, then quietly fade away, and again become a rare curiosity. This happened to the seaweed flies, which are always to be found on our beaches, but which suddenly came into the headlines of the newspapers in the autumn of 1953 because of their immense numbers, not only on the South Coast, but as far north as London and Oxford. Perhaps the weather of that year had something to do with it, but quite possibly the species was already due for a rise in numbers as part of its long-term fluctuation, and the warm autumn merely exaggerated this.

One cause of sudden increases of numbers of insects is our habit of planting big areas covered with one crop, because this provides the insects that feed on the plant with an unlimited supply of food, and a chance to increase more rapidly than their enemies. In time the enemies also increase, and restore a balance, but in the meantime the planter is likely to suffer heavy losses, and for financial reasons might be forced to give up trying to grow the crop. The planter's remedy is either to attack the insect with chemical insecticides, which gives quick results, but is expensive and will have to be repeated; or try to introduce other insects that will attack the pest, and perhaps control it permanently, by what is called *biological control*.

An illustration of this is the aphid *Therioaphis maculata*, which attacks clovers, lucerne and related leguminous plants in the U.S.A., Middle East and India. When these are planted as a fodder crop for feeding animals, 'The aphid reduces the hay-crop by feeding on the leaves, causing them to dry up and drop, by retarding the growth of the ... new shoots after the field is cut, and by killing some of the

Plate 55. Galls on turnip, cut open to show larvae of the turnip gall weevil, Order Coleoptera

A Shell Photograph

plants particularly, seedlings, and so thinning the stand. The copious honeydew secreted (see p. 107) complicates harvesting operations'. (Dickson and others, abstracted in *Review of Applied Entomology*, **A45**, p. 11.)

In Israel (Harpaz, same *Review*, p. 14) this same pest has about forty generations a year, and it is able to multiply very rapidly when it is presented with plenty of food, under good weather conditions. It is attacked by several insect enemies, lacewings, ladybirds and the larvae of hoverflies, but both in California and in Israel it was found that the increase of parasites lagged behind the increase of the aphid, and insecticides had to be used to keep the pest under control.

One of the most valuable field crops is cotton, which by its cultivation in big areas is much exposed to attack by insects. It was recently estimated that the annual loss through insects in the U.S.A. was well over 200 million dollars.

In spring the young plant is attacked by thrips (Thysanoptera) and aphids (Homoptera), which cause malformation and loss of foliage. The cotton flea-hopper (Heteroptera) reduces the number of fruiting branches. The boll-weevil (Coleoptera) is the most damaging pest of all, and lays its eggs in the flowers and fruit, where the larvae feed. The boll-worms are caterpillars of moths which destroy the boll (or fruit, with its coating of cotton fibres), whereas the leaf-worms are caterpillars of a tropical moth that flies in each year from the South. Other moths do minor damage.

A most important group of pests of cotton is the 'cotton-stainers', plant-feeding bugs (Heteroptera) which attack the bolls, causing the young ones to fall off, and the cotton lint in the older bolls to become discoloured. The leaves of the cotton-plant are damaged by a number of other insects of different Orders, as well as by red spider-mites.

To combat such a sequence of enemies, the cotton-planter must carry out a systematic programme of spraying through the year, but even then his losses may be substantial.

Biological Control

A classical example of biological control is that of the Coconut Moth, *Levuana iridescens*, in Fiji in the year 1925–6. The coconut is a long-lived tree, and once it is mature it normally produces a crop of nuts every month. The *Levuana* caterpillar eats the leaf, which gradually changes colour from a healthy green to brown, then to grey or white, and finally breaks away. After a tree has been completely stripped of

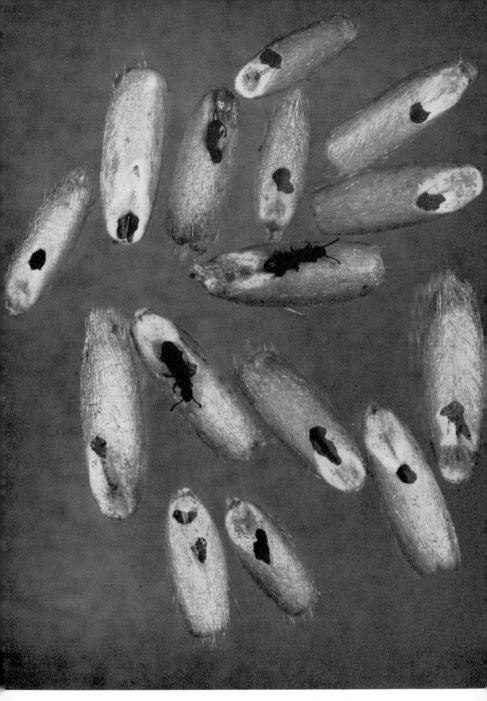

Plate 56. A grain-beetle, Order Coleoptera, and damaged grains

A Shell Photograph

leaves in this way it takes about two years to recover and bear fruit again.

Levuana had been present for many years on one island only of the Fiji group, called Viti Levu, and as a result it was not profitable to grow coconuts on that island. Occasionally the moth would spread temporarily to neighbouring islands, and by 1925 it was thought that there was a very serious risk that it would eventually spread throughout the Fiji group, where the growing of coconuts for copra was a flourishing, and indeed a vital activity. The threat of possible ruin to the copra estates was undermining the financial position of the islands.

It appeared that on Viti Levu the moth *Levuana* was established without any natural enemies that were capable of controlling it. The method of attack, therefore, was to try to find some other place where *Levuania* lived, and where it had enemies that might be introduced into Fiji. Strangely enough, this particular moth could not be found anywhere else. The fact that it was uncontrolled in Fiji suggested that this was not its natural home, and that it must previously have come from some other group of islands where it is now extinct.

In Malaya there were moths whose larvae had somewhat similar feeding habits, and which were heavily parasitised by a Tachinid fly, *Ptychomyia remota*. Infested larvae were transported to Fiji, and the adult flies that emerged from them were placed in cages with *Levuana* caterpillars, which they at once attacked. In less than three weeks a new generation of parasites had emerged and for six months parasitic flies were reared in this way in a laboratory, as well as being released in batches at intervals. At the end of that time it was possible to collect parasitised *Levuana* caterpillars on the coconut trees, showing that the parasite had established itself.

In a little over a year the *Ptychomyia* fly had exterminated the *Levuana* moth completely from the islands. Then came the question whether the fly could keep itself going by finding other food, or would it die out in turn. This was tested by taking *Levuana* caterpillars from the laboratory and exposing them on the trees, when they were at once attacked and parasitised. Thus not only was the pest eliminated, but there was an effective enemy waiting for it if any stray specimens should ever turn up again in the coconut groves.

A spectacular cure like this is very encouraging, but unfortunately circumstances are seldom so favourable, and apart from a few similar instances, biological control has not been an outstanding success. Either the parasites do not flourish on the insect pest, or, having done so, they spread to other hosts and become a pest in themselves. Biological control appeals to a biologist, because it is precise and elegant compared with the crude slaughter of insects by sprays, and if it is successful the control is likely to be lasting: but in the short view, to get a financial return in a particular year, it is often simpler just to spray.

Damage to Produce in Store

When a crop has been harvested it is often stored for months, or even for years, before being used, and while it is in store it is liable to be attacked by insects. A particular crop may suffer as much damage from insects while it is stored as it did while growing in the field (Plate 56).

Damage to stored produce is not so immediately obvious as that to a growing crop, because the produce is often in bales or other containers, or stored in bulk in a grain elevator. Because of the bulk and weight it is difficult to inspect for insect damage, and any method of sampling may easily miss pockets of infestation.

Insect damage to a growing crop may be offset by the vitality of the plant. A crop of strong plants, under good cultivation, may grow away to become immune to further attacks by a particular insect, and may even recover to some extent from attacks already made. Damage to stored produce cannot be retrieved. Moreover, if a growing crop is damaged this merely means that the farmer does not get as big a yield as he hoped: only in extreme cases, like the coconut moth we have mentioned is the loss likely to be complete. On the other hand stored produce has already a cash value, and every ton destroyed by insects is a direct monetary loss.

Estimates of the amount of the loss naturally vary greatly, according to the crop and to the climatic conditions under which it is stored. It has been said that up to 50% of the maize stored on North American farms may be destroyed by insects in some seasons, while many stored products suffer losses of more than 10%. The value of the stored grain lost annually in the U.S. is estimated at more than 500 million dollars, but the actual loss in practice is likely to be more than this. When a stock of grain has suffered damage by insects what is left has a lower market value, and some batches are likely to be scrapped entirely, because it is not worthwhile to sort out what is useable.

Insect damage to stored produce can be reduced, partly by prevention and partly by cure. Preventive measures are improved methods of storage to expose the produce less to insect invasion, and more thorough clearing up of the debris between one batch and another. Once the insect infestation is present the produce may be fumigated with poisonous gases, or treated with sprays, dusts and smokes. The great problem is to find chemicals that are effective against the insects, and yet do not make the produce harmful for human or animal consumption.

Plate 57. 'Glow-worm Cave', Waitomo, New Zealand, showing the luminous colony of *Arachnocampa luminosa* (Order Diptera) covering the roof

New Zealand Government Photograph

Bloodsucking Insects

Any insect that sucks the blood of man or of domestic animals is both a nuisance and a danger. The bite itself is often painful, though not always so. It used to be thought that the 'gadding' of cattle (when they run wildly about with tail in the air) was caused by the pain of being bitten by 'gad-flies', and though it is now believed that gadding is caused by non-biting insects, it is still true that cattle and horses in the fields may be kept in a restless state that lowers their condition and renders them more liable to other infections.

People, too, are tormented by large numbers of biting flies, and in the brief summer of the Arctic it may be impossible to move about out of doors without wearing special protective clothing against the attacks of hundreds of flies.

The immediate bite may not be painful, but it is often followed by a painful itching and swelling that lasts for several days. This is generally the result of the injection of saliva into the wound. The saliva of blood sucking insects contains a powerful anti-coagulin, which prevents the blood from clotting, and so blocking the mouthparts of the insect. It is this that produces the delayed symptoms after a bite.

The reaction that follows an insect-bite varies in different people, and in the same person under different conditions. Generally the first bite has little effect, but after a short interval the person becomes 'sensitised', and any further bites after that cause violent symptoms of swelling and pain. If the victim stays in the same area and goes on being bitten frequently, the effect gradually diminishes, until complete immunity is reached.

This is why people who have just arrived in an area often complain bitterly about the biting insects, whereas those who have been there some time say that they are never bitten. In fact they are, but they no longer show any reaction to the bites.

Transmission of Disease

Any insect that bites one person for a time and then flies off and immediately bites another is liable to carry the organisms of disease from one to the other. This is called mechanical transmission, because the insect's part is purely mechanical. You could get the same effect by sticking a hollow needle, first into one person and then into the other.

Mechanical transmission of disease is very probable in theory, but difficult to prove in practice. Usually we can only guess which insects probably carry the infection, because they are the most common on the animals concerned. Certain diseases of the eyes and skin in the tropics must clearly be spread by the flies that are seen settling on the affected areas.

Some of the most dangerous organisims of disease, however, spend a definite part of their life-cycle within the insect vector, or carrier, and indeed are unable to complete their growth and development without this alternative host. This sequence is called cyclical transmission, and the insect vector is an essential part of it.

By far the most important insect vectors of disease by cyclical transmission are the mosquitoes. The diseases they carry include malaria in all its forms; infections by parasitic worms called filariasis, of which elephantiasis (a grotesque swelling of the body) may be a result; yellow fever, and a number of other virus diseases (encephalitis and encephalo-myelitis), of which human 'sleepy sickness' is one. 'Sleeping sickness', on the other hand, is a different disease, caused by a trypanosome, a single-celled animal, which is cyclically transmitted in tropical Africa by the tsetse fly.

In each of these diseases the organism concerned is present in the blood of the person bitten, and is picked up by the biting insect. Inside the insect, the disease organism moves about through various organs, and finally reaches either the salivary glands or the cavities of the head near the base of the proboscis. During this migration, the organism changes shape, and develops into what is called an 'infective form', and when the insect bites another person, some of the infective forms are passed on to him, thus giving him the disease.

Thus an insect that has bitten an infected person is not able to pass on the disease to someone else until there has been time for the disease organism to develop into an infective form. This may take eight days for the malaria organism in a mosquito, or twenty days for the organism of sleeping sickness in a tsetse fly. From then onwards the fly may remain infective for most of its life.

In a similar way, the insects that suck the sap of growing plants play their part in spreading many serious diseases (see Carter, 1962).

Parasitic Insects

These are insects that do not merely attack man or other animals, but which remain attached to their 'host' for long periods. Fleas, lice and bed-bugs are external parasites; internal parasites include the maggots of various flies, such as the warble-fly of cattle, the bot-flies of horses and sheep, and the maggots of many other flies that may get into the human body more or less by accident.

Plate 58. Close-up of the hanging threads of the New Zealand Glow-worm, which are sticky and entrap small insects

New Zealand Government Photograph

Plate 59. Beneficial insects. An *Arum* is pollinated by small flies of the family Psychodidae. Photo by the late J. B. Bradbury

Fortunately, parasitic insects do not often carry human disease. Outstanding exceptions are plague, which is carried by a rat-flea and typhus carried by lice. Ticks carry a number of infections, but we can exclude these as not being insects, though in appearance and habits they conform more with the insects than with any other group of animals. The irritation set up by parasitic insects can be very debilitating, and the wounds and sores that they cause may easily become infected with bacteria. The maggots of some flies can be dangerous, because they are able to destroy so much of the living tissue of their host.

Beneficial Insects

It is easy to forget that there are 'good insects' as well as 'bad' ones. The honey-bee, the silkworm moth and the lac insect are obvious examples, where the insect produces something that we eagerly collect and use.

Perhaps the greatest benefit that we get from insects is their help in pollinating flowers. Not only honey-bees, but a great many wild bees, flies and other insects, go from blossom to blossom in search of nectar, and in doing so carry pollen from one plant to another. This is a more precise alternative to the wasteful method of relying on haphazard pollination by wind, and is the reason for the evolution of flowers. Everyone takes the beauty of flowers so much for granted that it is hard to realise that if there had never been any pollinating insects there would be no flowers. The flowering plants and the higher insects—especially Lepidoptera, Hymenoptera and Diptera—evolved together.

133

Plants have the advantage over most animals that they can often reproduce themselves vegetatively by splitting, or by sending out runners or rhizomes. Nevertheless, to remain vigorous and healthy they need the help of insects in cross-fertilisation. When an attempt is made to grow crops that are not native to an area it may be necessary to provide the insects to fertilise them: examples are sunflowers in East Africa, and alfalfa (lucerne) in Canada. Even in settled countries like England, where a balance has long been reached, there is a danger of upsetting it by using general insecticides, and weed-killers.

Many insects are enemies of man, but even more are enemies of other insects. We have mentioned how parasitic insects can be used in deliberate biological control of pests, but these examples are infinitesimal compared with the number that work away to our advantage all the time, without our being aware of it. Not only do insects control each other's numbers continually, but the insects also play an essential part in breaking up and disposing of dead animals, dung and refuse of all kinds. It is easy to turn away in disgust from the unsavoury habits of many insects, but they are doing an invaluable operation of clearing up, from which we benefit.

New Methods and New Problems

In the 1940s the development of DDT and other synthetic insecticides seemed to open a new era in the struggle against insects. These new chemicals were not only more poisonous to insects than ever before, but they also had the ability to retain their poisonous qualities indefinitely. It therefore seemed possible, at that time, that all noxious insects might be exterminated, at least over any area where they could do harm.

After a few years there was disquieting news that the new insecticides were not as effective as they had been, particularly against houseflies. 'Resistant strains' began to appear in different countries.

The development of resistance is a process of artificial selection akin to the Natural Selection by which evolution progresses. If a chemical spray or dust is used against a population of insects, and does not kill them all, the survivors will be of two kinds: those individuals that have escaped the spray by chance; and those individuals which happen to be naturally more resistant to the particular chemical in use. These survivors will breed, and the next generation will contain a higher proportion of resistant individuals. After a few applications, each killing off the weakest, the entire population will be descended from immune individuals: a *resistant strain.*

The usefulness of any chemical is therefore strongly limited by the development of resistant strains. Insects vary greatly in this ability, and unfortunately it is generally true that the insects most harmful to man are precisely those that are most likely to develop resistance. There is a reason for this. Those insects that have become pests are those which can modify their feeding habits to take advantage of the new habitats provided for them by man, his cultivated crops, the artificial conditions of his houses and towns, his domestic animals and himself. The same variability and versatility enables them to adapt themselves to chemical attack by developing a resistant strain.

The housefly is an example of this: it owes its unique position among pests to the ability of both adults and larvae to feed on a wide variety of substances, and hence to exploit the domestic scraps, refuse and waste everywhere produced by human habitation. This same versatility helps it to develop resistant strains.

A further objection to the 'wonder insecticides' of a few years ago is that very persistence that made them famous. Only lately has it been fully realised that if an insecticide does not decompose harmlessly, then successive small doses, insignificant in themselves, may build up over a period in crops, in stored food, in the bodies of animals and in man. Ideas of what is a dangerous dose at a single application have to be drastically modified, to take account of this build-up. Effects do not have to be lethal to matter; one example is the decline of some wild birds as a result of continual eating of chemically treated seed. This led to sterility, not only in the seed-eaters themselves, but also in the birds of prey that fed on them.

In search for alternative methods of attacking insects, one of the most promising is induced sterility: i.e. making the insects produce infertile eggs, or none at all. There are two methods of doing this, by the use of radiation, and by chemical means. In each case the scheme is to produce a large number of sterile males, which must, however, be normal in behaviour, so as to induce the females to complete their mating and egg-laying behaviour. If the number of sterile males greatly exceeds that of fertile males, the population will rapidly decline.

To do this by radiation means rearing males artificially, exposing them to gamma radiation, and releasing them among the wild population. This has been successfully accomplished in a few restricted areas, notably for screw-worm flies in the East Indian island of Curaçao. This method has the disadvantage that it can only be used for species that can be artificially reared in the laboratory, and that it requires access to radiation equipment.

A second method is to produce sterility by chemical means, spraying or dusting with chemical compounds that do not kill, nor alter behaviour but merely render the insects infertile. This has the big advantage that it can be used directly on the insect population, but of course it brings back some of the drawbacks inherent in chemical insecticides: how many other insects are also rendered sterile: what effect do the chemicals have on domestic animals and man?

The general lesson of all this is that attacks on insects must be controlled intelligently, and be suited to the locale, and to the particular pest. A sudden, powerful attack by a sequence of several methods, is safer and more likely to be effective than indiscriminate dustings with the same chemical over a period of time. A massive dose of insecticide may reduce the insect population to a low level temporarily, long enough for one of the other methods to have a chance of success.

In the meantime it must not be forgotten that the insects themselves are not inactive. The same versatility that is responsible for resistant strains also enables them to exploit quickly any new habitats provided for them by new activities of man. At this time the surface of the earth is being altered by man at a rate much greater than ever before, and far, far greater than the natural processes of climatic change in the past. Only the most versatile insects will be able to keep pace, but they will give a lot of trouble.

136

Not only will familiar pests like the housefly and some of the mosquitoes break out in new places, but entirely new pests will appear when insects have that hitherto been harmless, or even entirely unknown, will suddenly find conditions particularly favourable to them. In fact insect pests are often a direct result of man's own activities, and while modern societies are combating ancient diseases such as malaria they are opening our doors to other newer troubles. We hear a great deal nowadays about pollution by chemical contamination of the environment, but the physical presence of discarded objects, particularly those made of plastic, and relatively indestructible can present insects with attractive 'container habitats' in which they can breed.

Another problem is the speed of modern transport. Even in the old days of sailing ships certain domestic insects spread all over the world: the housefly, the bed-bug, and the human flea are examples of such 'cosmopolitan species'. Today people can travel from Europe to Australia in three days—less when we have supersonic airliners— and thousands cross the Atlantic every week. Not only is there more chance for harmful insects to survive the journey and escape at the other end, but there is also increased risk of human carriers of disease travelling to other countries where the local insects may bite them and pass on the disease into a new country.

One new opportunity for insects, perhaps a minor one, lies in the increased use of central heating in countries such as Britain where an equable climate formerly made this seem an extravagance. The spartan atmosphere of an English house has protected us against warmth-loving insects, with the exception of a few round the hearth, such a cockroaches, crickets and silverfish. Now that our buildings maintain a subtropical warmth all the year round we must look out for continuous breeding of house flies and blowflies (though our new addiction to deep freeze will discourage the latter), and we must always be on the watch for others that may come.

REFERENCES

BRITISH MUSEUM (NATURAL HISTORY), 1958. *A Handbook on Evolution*, pp. x + 100; figs.

BURR, MALCOLM, 1954. *The Insect Legion*. London: James Nisbet. 2nd Edn., pp. xvi + 336, figs. and pls.

CARTER, W., 1962. *Insects in Relation to Plant Disease*. New York and London. 705 pp., 175 figs.

CHAPMAN, R. F., 1969. *The Insects: structure and function*. London: English Universities Press. 819 pp., 509 figs.

CHAUVIN, R., 1967. *The World of an Insect*. London: World University Library. 254 pp., many figs.

HINTON, H. E., 1958. Concealed phases in the metamorphosis of insects. *Sci. Prog. London* 46(182): 260–275.

IMMS, A. D., 1957. *A General Textbook of Entomology, including the anatomy, physiology and classification of insects*. London: Methuen, 9th edn. Revised by O. W. Richards and R. G. Davies, pp. xii + 886, 609 figs.

——, 1971. *Insect Natural History*. London: Collins, *New Naturalist* series, pp. xviii + 317, 40 col. pls. 32 b/w pls., 40 text figs., 8 maps.

JOHNSON, C. G. 1969. *Migration and dispersal of insects by flight*. London: Methuen & Co. 763 pp., 210 figs.

MORETON, B. D., 1950. *Guide to British Insects: an aid to identification*. London: Macmillan, pp. viii + 188, 96 figs.

——, 1958. *Beneficial Insects*. Ministry of Agriculture Bulletin, No. 20. London: H.M.S.O.

NACHTIGALL, W., 1972. *Insects in Flight*. London: Allen & Unwin, 158 pp., 32 photographic plates, 59 text figs.

OLDROYD, H., 1964. *The Natural History of Flies*. London: Weidenfeld & Nicolson; N. York, W. W. Norton. 324 pp., 39 figs, 32 pls.

——, 1968. *Elements of Entomology: an introduction to the study of insects*. London: Weidenfeld & Nicholson; New York: Universe Books. 312 pp., 50 photographs, 72 text figs.

——, 1970. *Collecting, preserving and studying Insects*. London, Hutchinson, 2nd Edn. 336 pp., 10 pls., 135 figs.

PRINGLE, J. W., 1957. *Insect Flight*. Cambridge University Press, 133 pp., figs.

RIBBANDS, C. R., 1953. *Behaviour and Social Life of Honey-Bees*. London: Bee Research Assocn. 352 pp., 9 pls., figs.

ROSS, H. H. 1956., *A Textbook of Entomology*. New York: John Wiley, 519 pp., 402 figs.

References

ROYAL ENTOMOLOGICAL SOCIETY OF LONDON, 1949--. *Handbooks for the Identification of British Insects.* London: 41 Queen's Gate, S.W.7. For details apply to the Registrar at this address.

SNODGRASS, R. E., 1935. *Principles of Insect Morphology.* New York, 667 pp., figs.

SOUTHWOOD, T. R. E., 1966. *Ecological Methods: with particular reference to insect populations.* London: Methuen, 391 pp., 101 figs.

WATERHOUSE, D. F. and others, 1970. *The Insects of Australia.* Canberra: C.S.I.R.O., 1029 pp., many figs.

WIGGLESWORTH, V. B., 1953. *The Principles of Insect Physiology,* London: Methuen, 5th Edn. 554 pp., 355 figs.

WILLIAMS, C. B., 1958. *Insect Migration.* London: Collins, *New Naturalist* series, 225 pp., 8 col. pls., 16 b/w pls., 48 text figs.

INDEX

Index